TOO MUCH MONEY
IS NOT ENOUGH

★

TOO MUCH MONEY

★

IS NOT ENOUGH

★

Big Money and Political Power in Texas

★

SAM KINCH JR.

with Anne Marie Kilday

FOREWORD BY CHARLES LEWIS, CENTER FOR PUBLIC INTEGRITY

Library of Congress Cataloging-in-Publication Data

Library of Congress Catalog Number: 00-111170

ISBN: 1-893385-08-6

Printed in the United States of America

First Edition

12 11 10 9 8 7 6 5 4 3 2 1

5025 Burnet Road, #200
Austin, Texas 78756
1-512-472-1007

CONTENTS

★ ★ ★

FOREWORD

In this New Gilded Age of big money politics in which politicians everywhere are raising previously incomprehensible sums of campaign cash while steadfastly continuing the rhetorical charade that their powerful patrons have no influence on their public policies, truth and candor are endangered species. Let's be honest — our elected officials seldom have to answer for such folly, and on those rare occasions when they are asked a direct question about the special interest influence of a particular donor, they generally deflect, deny or even disappear. The non-responsive response has become all too familiar to us. Indeed, today we live in a substantially shame-free era in which "spin" and "damage control" are reverentially admired; they are "techniques" taught in colleges and universities. I remember when, not too long ago, it was called lying.

Against this mercenary milieu of mendacity, I was understandably skeptical when Fred Lewis (no relation) first mentioned this ambitious idea of talking to former members of the Texas Legislature about the sensitive subject of money in politics. But I am delighted to report that *Too Much Money Is Not Enough* is an important work that more than fulfills Fred's vision. Somehow, veteran journalists Sam Kinch Jr., and Anne Marie Kilday have managed to capture on these pages invaluable insights into the intersection of politics and commerce in Austin. And yes, we are afforded some extraordinary glimpses of those endangered species, truth and candor.

We forget sometimes how important our state legislatures are today. With billions and billions of dollars in federal money and new authority that has moved to the states as part of "devolution," life-and-death issues affecting the environment, and our health and safety, are decided in state capitals across the country. Health insurance and education, two of the hottest public concerns today, are substantially decided at the state and local level. In 1999, 25,031 bills were enacted into public law in state legislatures across America, and state governments collected more than $470 billion from us, according to StateNet.

Most of this activity generally is, to be blunt, poorly covered by the news media and largely ignored by the public. We should all be paying much more attention to our state lawmakers, their policies and their hidden agendas. Beyond the usual influence of campaign contributions, 41 out of the 50 state legislatures are run by part-timers who meet a few months a year, and draw salaries that average about $18,000 annually. Some of the most populous states leave the public interest to career lawyers, bankers, farmers, lobbyists and insurance brokers in the legislature.

In *Too Much Money Is Not Enough*, we learn how much money and maneuvering surround the Texas legislature, which is fascinating since it only meets every other year and its members are among the lowest paid legislators in the nation, with an annual salary of $7,200. Obviously, the power, the glory and the rationale for being a state legislator lie elsewhere. Rife with conflicts of interest, in 1998, 33 percent of Texas lawmakers sat on legislative committees that regulated their professional or business interest, and 50 percent had financial ties to businesses or organizations that lobby state government.

The most disturbing problem of all, in Texas and around the U.S., is the incestuous relationship between lawmakers and their most powerful patrons. We all understand the old line about dancing "with them that brung you." Well, today 97 percent of Texas citizens do not contribute to any state politicians, and 96 percent of the American people don't give a dime to any politician or party. Very, very few people sponsor our politicians today, and they represent economic interests with business before government.

The tragedy of it all is that most Texans, most Americans, know very little about politics today. Most cannot name their elected representatives in Austin or in Washington, let alone what is really going on "behind closed doors." It is long past time for that to change. These are our employees, public servants entrusted to do the public's business.

Abraham Lincoln once said, "I am a firm believer in the people. If given the truth, they can meet any national crisis. The great point is to bring them the real facts." *Too Money Much Is Not Enough* provides some of the "real facts" today about Texas politics, including some wonderfully candid admissions by lawmakers about the price of power.

Charles Lewis is the founder and executive director of the Center for Public Integrity in Washington, and author of *The Buying of the President 2000* (Avon Books).

I

"If you would persuade, first you must appeal to interest rather than intellect."

— *From Benjamin Franklin, American founding father and journalist–turned–politician/diplomat*

★   ★   ★

WHY ARE WE TELLING THIS STORY?

Nearly 30 years ago, while still a full-time political reporter, I co-authored "Texas Under a Cloud," about the 1971-72 Sharpstown stock-fraud scandal that provoked the last great political upheaval in the state. That book was a best-seller, at least by then-prevailing Texas standards for non-fiction, and was used as the basis for an untold number of successful and unsuccessful "reform" campaigns by individuals and groups in the 1972 general election. Lots of things have changed for the better since then, including the passage of a 1973 campaign-finance reporting law by a "reformed" Legislature, nearly half of whose members were new to their jobs. But one constant is the simple truth that political money — private contributions to candidates, their causes and their parties — still dictates governmental results in Texas pretty much as it did in pre-"reform" days. And the Texas campaign finance reporting law really hasn't changed much in the last three decades, except for the Legislature's 1999 decision to make campaign-finance reports available on the Internet.

★ ★ ★

History tells us, to be sure, that the election process has been remarkably the same since a bunch of former colonial subjects revolted against a distant king and embarked on an unprecedented exercise in representative self-government. As much as we sometimes idealize yesteryear's politics and politicians, our leaders have always been elected in the same basic way: They think there is public support for them, they ask their friends to speak well of them and they raise money to get their message to voters beyond their circle of friends' friends. The way the message is delivered has changed, and the cost has gone up, but the process hasn't changed. If you expect to get elected, and particularly if you want to get **re-elected**, you have to make more than friends. You must be rich, as George Washington was, or pretend to be, as

Thomas Jefferson did, or you have to rely increasingly on Other People's Money, the sine qua non of politics.

You can bet, too, that the cost of political poker continues to rise. During the 1995-1996 election cycle, the presidential race and all campaigns for the U.S. Senate and U.S. House cost a combined $2 billion. True, 1997-1998's total was lower because only U.S. Senate and House campaigns were on the ballot. But, it is estimated that the year 2000 elections will have cost a combined $3.5 billion, as the total from so-called "soft money" giving and spending at least doubled.

On top of that, campaigns nationwide for state-level executive positions, chiefly governor, and for the state legislatures add at least another $1 billion in each election cycle. In Texas, less than two decades ago, a two-year election cycle that included campaigns for governor and most other executive-branch offices, and for the Legislature, cost less than $20 million. In more recent two-year election cycles, $100 million was closer to the mark; it was a minimum of $121 million in the 1997-98 cycle. And that didn't include the every-10-years cost run-up that occurs just before and right after the decennial census, as the major political parties vie for control of state legislatures during the post-census re-districting period.

★   ★   ★

Remember from your civics books, too, that money, while it is not the root of all evil, has only increased in importance in politics to the extent that there is more demand for it and more options to spend it. (As an undergraduate major in political history, I learned the old adage that "every time they hold an election, the price goes up.") Dozens of years ago or decades ago (take your pick), it was cheaper to run for office because the expenses were lower in dollars, and because ways to spend money were not as many. The old-fashioned printing press, which is now mostly confined to museums, was the biggest consumer of political money in the "good old days," when-ever those were, followed by billboards, other outdoor signs, hand-out fliers and push-cards. In the modern era, advertising via tightly targeted direct (bulk) mail and via the electronic media —TV and radio, predominantly, but also the Internet with its updated-daily and interactive capability — has become not just standard but a requirement for almost all credible political campaigns, and along with the various other means of voter contact — from serious telephone polls to **measure** voter sentiment to phony "push polls" on ways to **move** voter sentiment—have added options to the voter-contact mandate. As with carry-out pizza, each option has its cost.

There still are some "grassroots" campaigns for the Legislature, but they are few and far between enough to prove the point: Even being elected to the Texas Senate or Texas House now costs far more than it did just a few cycles in the past. And, as legislative districts become increasingly dominated by urban-area population, which has been happening for five decades, the cost of running in those districts also goes up. It's not usual, but a hot campaign between well-financed Democratic and Republican candidates in a big-city House district that is closely balanced between the parties can easily cost $600,000 or more. And $1 million, on both sides, for a Senate district campaign in a rural area is now closer to the norm, with big-city districts and districts that cover both urban and rural populations costing two to three times that much.

★ ★ ★

However, another factor can't be overlooked in the consideration of political money. The polls tell us people have the vision and the dream of what they want in government, but statistically they don't give enough of a damn to vote for or contribute to or otherwise support candidates for public office. And a sometimes reliable fact is that, at least in this instance, the statistics don't lie: Voter participation, at all levels of government, is at or near the lowest levels in the nation's history (except for World War II, when 20 million Americans moved away from home for work or training). Folks all over the world are clamoring, even fighting, for what they perceive as our version of an elective system of government. Yet, we aren't even doing **here** what they say they want **elsewhere**.

Remember that we're talking, in this context, only about the vote-getting behavior of politicians, rather than the ways they govern once elected or, heaven help us, re-elected. To paraphrase the humorist and commentator Will Rogers, who died in 1935, if we have public officials who can't or won't vote independently of their contributors, we don't have to keep re-electing them. Nevertheless, we usually do. In Texas and most states, 80 to 85 percent of incumbent legislators seeking re-election win another term; 85 to 90 percent of the time, the best-financed candidate wins the election; and when an incumbent also is the best-financed candidate, his victory probability goes above 95 percent, wherever he lives. In the 1998 Texas House races, too, the average incumbent received $2.50 in contributions for every $1 collected by a challenger; not surprisingly, then, winning incumbents collectively outspent their losing challengers by a remarkably similar margin of 2 to 1.

*   *   *

Yes, there is always the fact of incumbency. Those who are in charge of making the law seldom are receptive to changing anything in the law that currently benefits them. The present Texas campaign-finance law cannot, in anyone's perspective, be seen as anything other than protecting incumbency. Indeed, as seen through the eyes of anyone who is not a stake-holder in the process — stake-holders here defined as those who give to and work for the election of candidates for public office in the state—the current law all but demands the re-election of incumbents.

It should come as no surprise to anyone that those economic interests with the most at financial stake in state government contribute the most money to Texas campaigns. (Don't throw a textbook at me. We all have economic interests at stake in state government, but most of us either don't realize it or can't afford to do much about it.) Nor should it be a shock that those with the most at stake are organized in their political actions. The simple explanation is to say that "the lobby" dictates where most campaign money goes, but, as is true of many explanations, that is too simple: All of the economic interests affected by state government aren't truly organized by lobby groups, though most are. Many of those interests are business and professional groups, whose members typically have what is loosely called a trade association; many, if not most, of those groups also have political action committees (PACs), to which group members contribute and from which individual candidates receive campaign money. But, some of the interest groups are a bit more complicated. Individual labor unions may have their own lobbyists and PACs, for example, in addition to the Texas AFL-CIO, which includes most unions in the state and has its own PAC. And the Texas Trial Lawyers Association has its own lobby and PAC operation, while many trial-lawyer firms also lobby and make political contributions independently. In the same way, a major Texas company may belong to several trade associations and give to their PACs (say, the Texas Chemical Council, the Texas Association of Business and Chambers of Commerce and the Texas Civil Justice

League)—yet, at the same time that employer-company maintains its own lobby team and PAC.

Historically, "the lobby" — using this more expansive sense — actively participated in the political process from the grassroots level up. If a group of independent insurance agents could find and elect a representative, it did so. The candidate was recruited locally, but his campaign then would find a willing donor in the agents' statewide trade association. The same thing happened for a power company or a group of lawyers or a segment of the business community. Once elected, a state official's future depended on some variation of the "friendly incumbent" rule. That rule dictated, and still does to a large extent, that an interest group continue to support an incumbent with a voting record friendly to its interests. In recent years, that rule has been extended to a somewhat broader standard: Business groups, in general, support an incumbent whose voting record in totality is pro-business. Anyone who follows campaign finances in legislative races, for example, will notice quickly that most business groups contribute to the same candidates. Another development in recent years is the changing dynamics of party affiliation: While Republicans in the Legislature are, on the whole, more pro-business, that doesn't mean business groups automatically contribute to a Republican challenger. If that GOP challenger is running against a Democrat with a "friendly incumbent" voting record, the incumbent usually gets most of the business lobby money.

★   ★   ★

The lobby may be hard to follow in some ways, but its tracks are large. In the 1997-98 statewide and legislative campaign cycle, of the $121 million contributed to all candidates, $55 million came from political action committees — and $32 million of that came from corporate, law firm or other professional PACs. The other $23 million was from general business PACs, ideological and single-issue PACs and a smaller fraction from labor union PACs.

Take a look at the 1998 Texas House races. Half of all the money spent in all districts came from just 10 ZIP codes, and one-third of all money spent on House races came from just two ZIP codes in Austin, which is headquarters to most of the business trade-association PACs and almost all of the PAC-affiliated lobbyists. The number hasn't been updated for the subsequent election, but in all 1996 House elections an average of 80 percent of the money came from outside the district of the recipi-ent-candidate. (It is true, however, that a business might have a plant or a store or some other presence in the candidate's district, but the business PAC was located in Austin.) A handful of representatives receive almost all of their money from outside their districts, a fact that few of their constituents know.

Some more perspective on how Texas politics isn't exactly the common man's sport: For all of the 1998 statewide and legislative campaigns only 629 individuals and PACs contributed almost exactly half of the $121 million. Also, 55 percent of all givers contributed $1,000 or more, yet half of all the money came in checks of $25,000 or more. Less than 5 percent of the money came from checks of $500 or less. And from a professional fund-raiser comes this tidbit: Only 300 individual Texans contributed more than $10,000. Another bit of perspective: 97 percent of Texans, if they are typical of the country as a whole, **will never make a reportable contribution** to a candidate for public office. Of course, it's entirely possible that "Joe Six-pack" feels it is somewhat more important to feed, clothe and house his family than to help some politician pursue his bliss.

Wow!

* * *

On the other hand, it isn't always easy to follow the political money because Texas has one of the nation's least effective campaign-finance reporting laws. That is the focus of this book, to see what might be done to make the law more effective in terms of letting the ordinary citizen find out who is financing campaigns in Texas, and why and how that financing affects the government he gets from his own elected offi-cials. It's not a bang-'em-on-the-head approach; I have too much respect for the prac-titioners of Texas politics, including those in the lobby, to engage in a diatribe. Rather, we look at some holes in the law and consider some alternative ways to plug those holes.

Perhaps I should have included one other proposal: State law should require a winning candidate to submit his sworn campaign finances to a binding audit by the state to determine whether his campaign accurately, timely, and completely account-ed for all contributions and expenditures. The subsequent penalty for perjury would be automatic removal from public office and a ban on holding office in the future. Of course, there could be some downside to that law.

* * *

This book is written from the Jeffersonian perspective that the people of Texas care about state policy and politics, about who is elected to state office and why, about who pays for the campaigns and why. But, Thomas Jefferson's body of written work assumes something fundamental that is missing in today's political climate: He believed that a **well-informed** electorate was fully capable of making decisions about representation in a republican form of government. The fact is that the voters of Texas are not well-informed about who finances the campaigns of the folks they elect. State campaign-finance law doesn't require enough information for even the few well-intended, committed news media to do the job thoroughly, much less for "Joe Six-pack" himself to do it.

A demurrer: The title of the book may sound like a play on a popular country-western song from a few years ago (the key line of which was, "Too much is not enough of your love"). In fact, the phrase was used by a former legislator, now a lobbyist, in an off-the-record explanation of the attitude of most incumbent legislators when they seek ever-more, ever-larger campaign donations, even if they have little or no electoral opposition to speak of: "We (contributing lobbyists) may think they are asking for too much, but they always tell us that too much isn't enough to avoid the prospect of defeat, either now or in the future." I think that pretty well sets up this story.

The data in this work are an amalgam of efforts, including the simple math of the author. But the heavy lifting of data collection, verification, and analysis was done by non-profit organizations, including most prominently the National Institute on Money in State Politics (www.followthemoney.org), the Center for Responsive Politics (www.opensecrets.org), Texans for Public Justice (www.tpj.org), the Center for Public Integrity (www.publicintegrity.org), the Annenberg Center for Public Policy at the University of Pennsylvania (www.appcpenn.org) and the Committee for the Study of the American Electorate (www.gspm.org).

The interviews that follow Chapter 6 are designed to reflect some, but obviously by no means all, of the attitudes of former Texas legislators toward both the act of fund-raising and the reporting of its results. Anne Marie Kilday, a former colleague and competitor in the Capitol press corps, conducted the interviews that appear more or less intact, and also provided me with reality-based advice and comfort in the preparation of the rest of the text.

Sam Kinch Jr.
Austin, Texas
September 1, 2000

2

"**Obviously in the court system, it's particularly bad,
(because) people are taking money
while they are trying cases
and could be making rulings on them (contributors).**"

— *From former Rep. John Hirschi, D–Wichita Falls, on campaign–finance law as it relates to the judiciary*

★ ★ ★

A SEPARATE DEAL FOR THE JUDGES

Before moving to the broader subject, it should be noted briefly that the campaign-finance law for judicial candidates is different from and in some ways better than that affecting other state officials for the most basic reason: Both trial lawyers and defense counsel were appalled at the cost and the nastiness of the 1994 Democratic primary for the Supreme Court between Raul Gonzalez, the conservative defense-counsel candidate, and Rene Haas, the liberal trial-lawyer candidate. The two legal factions agreed on the need for some restraint, and so did many equally appalled judges and former judges. In addition, a general stench had been attached to the Texas judiciary for several years after a CBS "60 Minutes" TV program suggested that judges here were being "bought" by lawyer-contributors who had cases pending before or on the way to the Supreme Court. In the 1995 legislative session, a judicial-reform lobby organization, headed by former Chief Justice John L. Hill, whose main goal was changing the way judges are selected, and several good-government groups — notably Common Cause, Public Citizen of Texas and the League of Women Voters — combined to help pass the separate campaign-finance law for judicial races. (By law, incumbent judges were restricted in what they were allowed to tell the Legislature, collegially and publicly, about what they supported or opposed, but Supreme Court Chief Justice Tom Phillips was an out-front cheerleader for the cause.)

One can argue cynically that the 1995 Judicial Campaign Fairness Act doesn't matter much, anyway, because only lawyers really are involved in that part of the election process. But election law is supposed to matter to every citizen, and the separate statute applying to judicial candidates also is important for both what it does do and what it doesn't do. Moreover, in the last two decades, non-lawyers increasingly have become involved as contributors to judicial campaigns. And, most basically, many of us don't avail ourselves of the opportunity, but all Texans can vote on their judicial selections — even if they vote blindly, such as by partisan affiliation, or stupidly, such as by a candidate's catchy or famous name.

★   ★   ★

Here are the most important things that the Judicial Campaign Fairness Act requires:

• Aggregate expenditures are limited to $2 million for each statewide election, with lower amounts for non-statewide judgeships depending on the size of the judicial district.

• Contributions from individuals are limited to $5,000 for each statewide election, with lower amounts for non-statewide judgeships depending on the size of the judicial district.

• Law firms and PACs can give no more than $30,000 in each statewide election, and general-purpose PACs cannot give more than 15 percent of a candidate's total contributions.

• A contributor must be identified not only by name and address, but by principal occupation and job title, plus the full name and business address of the contributor's employer or law firm.

The most obvious flaw in the judicial campaign-finance law — other than the fact that it applies only to judicial races —is that the expenditure limit is voluntary. A candidate does not have to comply with the legal limits if any one of his opponents does not comply. The limit on contributions, by contrast, is screwed up enough to scream madly for judicial interpretation or legislative correction. Simply put, if one candidate says he won't comply with the law, the contribution limit becomes mandatory for him alone — but other candidates in the same race are then not bound by the contribution limit even if they'd already said they would comply. In hundreds of judicial elections in the two cycles since the law was adopted, however, the voluntary law has been complied with in all but two races (both for district judgeships in South Texas).

The other major, though not so obvious, flaw in the judicial campaign-finance law is that the contribution and expenditure limits are per election. That means if a statewide judicial candidate faces a contested primary, a primary run-off and a general-election race, he can raise up to $15,000 from individuals and $90,000 from law firms and PACs and spend up to $6 million in an election year. Another, lesser flaw is that the law still allows incumbent judges, with no opposition from either party, to raise and spend money up to the statutory limits for a primary and a general election, and the Legislature hasn't seen fit to change that. (In the summer of 2000, Republican Justice Priscilla Owen returned to her contributors about $103,000 of the $295,000 that she raised after she attracted no opponents in either major party and thus had no primary opponent.) Finally, the so-called purists in the campaign-finance reform camp argue that the judicial candidate statute is good in that it limits when a candidate can raise campaign money. But they complain that it has no requirement that, once elected, a judge recuse himself from cases before his court in which he accepted campaign donations from one or both of the parties and/or their lawyers. That might create havoc in the courts — particularly in the multi-judge appeals courts — but it would be more realistic to require that a judge disclose in each case, before it goes to trial, whether he has taken campaign money from any of the parties or their lawyers. It's supposed to be a matter of public record, anyway, but the argument is that the public would feel more comfortable knowing that its judges aren't unreasonably influenced by campaign contributions.

★   ★   ★

The 1995 statutory change hasn't driven lawyers' money out of judicial campaigns, of course. Texans for Public Justice, a trial lawyer-oriented non-profit study group, found that the nine justices on the Texas Supreme Court raised just over $11 million between 1994 and 1998. Of that amount, 48 percent came from lawyers and law firms and 15 percent more of it from the two political action committees of the biggest tort-reform organizations, Texas Civil Justice League and Texans for Lawsuit Reform. Moreover, while the justices elected in 1994 (before the law was changed) received only 35 percent of their campaign money from lawyers and law firms, the justices elected in 1998 received 57 percent of their money from the same source. The TCJL and TLR have proposed reforms, many of them already adopted, to restrict plaintiffs' damage awards from, or even to prohibit litigation of, certain types of personal-injury cases in Texas — thus helping the economic interests of some business and professional people but harming the economic interests of plaintiffs and personal-injury trial lawyers. The Texans for Public Justice study indicated that, of the $5.2

million in lawyer and law-firm contributions to the winning justices (all of them Republicans) on the Supreme Court, 79 percent came from business and insurance defense attorneys and 13 percent from plaintiffs' lawyers. The study also said that 96 percent of the money contributed to the nine justices came in checks larger than $100.

This is not a trivial matter: A survey done for the Supreme Court three years ago found that almost all lawyers and even a majority of judges in Texas think campaign contributions influence the courts' decisions.

3

"I did have to go to the hospital emergency room for stitches to close the wound, but it wasn't life-threatening. Redistricting can get pretty emotional."

— *From former Rep. Paul Ragsdale, D–Dallas, on cutting his hand during a table–pounding discussion about redistricting when a proposed map was on a glass table in the Speaker's Office*

★   ★   ★

POLI SCI 101:
POLITICIANS CHOOSING THEIR VOTERS

One of the nasty secrets of Texas legislative and congressional politics is that only one election cycle in a decade is really competitive between the two major parties—the first election after redistricting—and, thanks to technology, even that one cycle is becoming less of a mystery. Under the Texas constitution, redistricting is the way the Legislature exposes itself in the worst sense: The 150 members of the House draw their own districts to reflect growth and changes in population distribution in the most recent census, and the 31 members of the Senate do the same with their districts. (Historically, one body doesn't mess with the other body's districts; all kinds of internecine warfare would erupt if the House tried to change Senate districts, or vice versa.)

Surprise, citizens! Those incumbent legislators don't draw districts with the voters' interests or the political scientists' approval in mind. Bound only by constitutional restraints and those of the Voting Rights Act, they draw maps that tend to help themselves most of all and to help their party as a strong yet secondary consideration. For that reason, squiggly lines, skinny snake-like meanderings and maps worthy of a Rorschach Test are the rule rather than the exception. Often, one district is drawn solely to include an incumbent's house, while another is drawn solely to protect another incumbent by excluding a likely challenger's house. One might reasonably ask how that fine a detail can be included in a redistricting map covering 15 million or so eligible voters in 254 counties and more than 10,000 political units (including election precincts), and the answer is technology.

*　*　*

A Texas Legislative Council computer system that does the actual map-drawing has more political data in it than the average citizen can conceive. Imagine that you live in an urban area with a reasonable approximation of Texas' population proportions. The TLC computer can not only draw a map of a House district within that area, but can lead you to surmise how the district is likely to vote on the basis of how the election precincts within it have voted in the past. In addition, the computer delivers such demographic information as how many anglo, black, and brown voters there are, how they are united or divided by age, income and voter registration, and whether a given block or group of blocks in a neighborhood are primarily owner-occupied or rented houses, etc.

Redistricting is typically so litigated by the political parties as well as by minorities that, in Texas at least, it's not unusual for the Legislative Council's computer to be used in federal courts' re-drawing of districts, too. The upshot is the same, in that both the parties and the interested candidates know pretty well in advance how the districts are likely to perform in actual elections. However, politics is a contact sport, so elections have to be held before there is any certainty that the computer analysis is right. Fortunately for us, the "contact" part of the political game still requires a contest before you have a winner. And, just as a block party will be successful in some neighborhoods but not in others, so legislative districts do not always follow the pro forma that a computer yields.

Furthermore, for that first election after redistricting, incumbency is not as much of a predictable winning factor as it is in subsequent elections from the same district. The fact is, even an incumbent must nearly always run in some unfamiliar territory — the parts of the new district that were not in his old district. You can expect electoral surprises when, for example, a challenger who lives in a new part of the district runs and wins in that new part, but also gets enough votes from the old part of the district to unseat the incumbent. This is the way the political player learns whether a district that had been predictably Democratic, for example, has turned Republican in the last 10 years or whether, if the district remains Democratic, it has become conservative rather than moderate-liberal. There are exceptions, obviously, and in a mobile and growing state like Texas, neighborhoods change during a decade and so do election districts. The most visible macroscopic change of the 1980s and 1990s, for example, was the urban-to-suburban movement of white Democrats, who increasingly turned Republican when they moved. But the fact is, most districts become predictable after that first round of elections under the new lines, and that further reduces the competitiveness of the political process during the next election cycles.

★　★　★

We have been talking here about Texas legislative districts, because that is the chief focus of this book. But the same fundamentals are true of congressional districts, which also are drawn by legislators. The big difference is that the House and the Senate draw their own, separate congressional district maps, then settle the differences in a conference committee whose statewide map becomes law unless vetoed by the governor or over-ruled by one or more federal judges. (If a Texas House or Senate member is interested in running for Congress, as some inevitably are, this is where you most easily spot the fox guarding the hen house: There isn't anything subtle about a Texas legislator trying to draw a congressional district that he thinks he can win.) Again, whether the Legislature's version of a map or a federal court's is used, the first election usually tells the avid political watcher how the state's new congressional districts are likely to perform.

The rule about incumbency is the same for members of Congress as for members of the Legislature — perhaps even more so, because congressmen have larger staffs and budgets: Incumbents win about 85 percent of the time. The incumbent is usually the best-financed candidate, and the incumbent who is best-financed has about a 95 percent probability of being re-elected.

★　★　★

All of this is why, in turn, in a typical political season **after that first round** of post-redistricting elections, only 10 to 15 percent of all legislative districts are truly competitive. Incumbency is one big part of that, and fund-raising is the other. The latter, as we shall see, is closely related to and heavily influenced by the former. In 1998, the most recent year for nearly all of the data in this book, Republicans retained a majority in the Texas Senate, 16 to 15, though they lost the seat held by Sen. Michael Galloway, R-The Woodlands, defeated by Democrat David Bernsen of Beaumont, who raised three times as much money. In the House, Democrats retained a 78-72 majority, although they lost four seats to the GOP. More significant, for our purposes, is that of the 16 Senate races and the 150 House races, **97 percent of the winners were incumbents or raised the most money or both.** Only five legislative candidates in all of those legislative campaigns won without the advantage of incumbency or the advantage of having the most money.

As noted above, the next actually fully competitive legislative elections won't be held until the year 2002, after redistricting is done in 2001 either by the Legislature, the Legislative Redistricting Board or the federal courts. But in both 1998 and 2000, the national parties spent millions of dollars in attempting to win more Republican or Democratic Texas House and Senate seats precisely because of redistricting. Remember, the 1998 election cycle total for Texas legislative races was a candidate-reported $32.9 million.

4

"No person who has any sense about what's right
and wrong in this world will believe that kind of money
($100,000 from a specific group) doesn't influence a vote.
And it does. If it does nothing else, it creates the appearance.
And that appearance alone is cause for concern,
because it is the public's trust in the government
that is at stake here."

—— *From former Rep. Mike Martin, D–Galveston, on different views of political money*

★　★　★

Voting w/ th not the ballot

IT'S THE MONEY THAT MATTERS

A reasonable person asks why it is true that campaign cash and incumbency are such political soul mates. It's a fairly simple two-part answer: a) Money talks in politics, literally, and the language of money is spoken more sweetly to and by incumbents. b) With some exceptions, voters are more likely to be familiar with an elected official who has a taxpayer-financed staff. But, even for a neophyte who has never held public office, the availability of money is a critical, if not the overwhelming, factor in his viability as a candidate. If the candidate doesn't have the big bucks in his own bank account or doesn't have friends who will give enough up-front cash to "seed" the campaign, it's difficult to pay the bills for office rent, a minimal staff, telephone and other communications gear, printing and postage. And, that catalog of expenses comes before buying push cards, bumper stickers, yard signs, etc. — and before even considering the purchase of newspaper, radio, and TV advertising time.

A political player who looks at a neophyte's campaign will make sure that some amount of money is in the bank or in sight before investing the player's own time and money. That in itself can have a chilling effect on political campaigns: If a primary requirement for a candidate is to have or be able to raise campaign money, the otherwise well-qualified prospective public official may decide to sit on the sidelines and, therefore, the voters are deprived of his potential competition. Another perspective: If the lack of up-front money discourages the donation of later money, it becomes a death spiral in which the person of modest means, whose friends also aren't well-off, is the loser before the contest starts.

★   ★   ★

An incumbent, on the other hand, usually has no such worries. Even if he has served just one term in office, he ordinarily will have a public record that persuades at least an individual, an interest or a group that the incumbent is worthy of re-election. (That can cut both ways, of course: The same record that appeals to some may repel others, who are just as persuaded to help a challenger.) But the incumbent legislator, for example, already has realized how the campaign bread is buttered because he won that first election; the only remaining issue is where to get the bread and the butter for the next election.

As an incumbent, though, he routinely will have developed relations, good or bad, with various Austin lobbyists. Those lobbyists make their living by influencing public policy in the Legislature and state agencies. Those lobbyists may not contribute much of their own money, but they do direct, or at least influence, contributions from their clients. A legislator, for instance, may not have a 100 percent voting record on behalf of a given industry, but he's likely to get money from those interests if he voted "right," say, two-thirds of the time. His support record might not need to be that high, however, if he is a member of a House or Senate committee that handles most of a special interest's affairs.

$$\star \quad \star \quad \star$$

The Austin business and professional lobby has a long tradition of holding "receptions" for legislative candidates who want to meet-and-greet the folks who either give or persuade their clients to give money to candidates. All it takes is a call to a single friend, or a friend of a friend, in the lobby, who then schedules a time and date for an event, most of which are held at the Austin Club. (Most lobbyists are members there; it's located in downtown near the Capitol and it's convenient to the major hotels. It's also clubby enough that plebeians don't drop in by mistake.) For a variety of reasons, mostly inclusiveness, all interested lobbyists are on a list of potential invitees to these receptions, and on the omnibus faxed notice of a time and date, and are given a chance to be listed as "sponsors" (which requires paying a share of the cost, not promising a contribution). Typically, these are two-hour cocktail parties at which a candidate is introduced to or becomes re-acquainted with lobbyists who might be helpful in paying for the candidate's campaign. The candidate also is given a chance to discuss his attitudes toward possible or likely legislative issues. When the reception is over, the candidate also is given a copy of the sign-in sheet that tells him who attended. The first-time candidate may not walk away with a pocketful of money, but at least he has made some contacts for possible future donations. For the incumbent, the lobby reception is more clearly a fundraising event and is more pre-dictably successful. Indeed, during a political season, an incumbent might hold more than one such event, although lobbyists resist a legislator who tries to go to the well too often and, thus, appears greedy.

* * *

It's true that legislators, or even candidates for the Legislature, can't take money for their votes or promises of votes. That's illegal. But the law doesn't say that a can-didate or an incumbent, in the process of raising campaign money, can't spell out his attitude toward, even a detailed position on, a specific approach to public policy. Indeed, that is a fairly typical pattern for an incumbent, at least, because he is more likely to be informed in advance about what the special interest at hand would like to see done. For at least the 40 years that I have watched Texas politics, that is part of the process, not just part of the lore. And, if a neophyte candidate for the Legislature wants (wisely) to avoid the specifics about future legislation, but still raise special-interest money, he will instead use a generic but clear-cut code phrase like "I am pro-actively pro-business."

* * *

It is not a criticism of this kind of fund-raising to note that the lobbyist and his clients are not likely to be residents of the district in which the legislator serves. Indeed, while the first-time legislative candidate may raise nearly all of his first-elec-tion money from within the district, an average of 80 percent of it probably will come from outside the district in future election campaigns. Whatever the proportion or the source, however, one thing is clear about lobby money for legislative incumbents: Both sides know why the cash is flowing. It flows from one who wants something done to one who wants to be re-elected, and neither is likely to forget the other. And keep in mind that statistic from earlier: For $1 a Texas challenger actually raises, an incumbent typically raises $2.50. (Note that I said "actually raises" to distinguish from the self-financed candidate's contributions to his own campaign; candidate self-finance totaled $8.9 million in 1998 legislative races.)

What logically follows, then, is that the public is left out of this knowledge — unless the news media do their jobs or the incumbent's challenger does his. That is a

long row of cotton to hoe under the current disclosure law. Nailing down the economic identity of contributors and analyzing the reports is liable to be expensive and
time-consuming as a project for anyone, and there is no certainty that the project
would produce a smoking gun, anyway. Voters may yawn at the results, whether published in a newspaper or used in a stump speech by the challenger. Yet campaign
money obviously matters — people wouldn't be giving and getting so much of it otherwise. Keep in mind that in 1998, legislative winners spent $25.6 million, while gen-
eral-election losers spent $5.7 million. Another $1.5 million was spent by those who
lost their primary campaigns.

5

**"The question you really need to ask members
is not whether they remember that you gave to them,
but whether they can remember who gave to their opponents.
They can all recite that. They know that list, by heart.
That one they carry to the grave."**

— *From former Rep. Bruce Gibson, D–Godley, on the duality of giving*

★   ★   ★

WHO GIVES AND WHY?

I t's debatable, of course, but it can be argued that the fairly recent rise of Democratic-vs.-Republican competition caused the tremendous increase in the cost of Texas politics. For generations, after all, the main competition in our elections was between the long-dominant conservative segment of the Democratic Party and the generally woebegone liberal wing of Democrats. Conservatives had plenty of major and mid-level contributors and, thus, often two conservatives would battle in a primary to get into a run-off against the chronically under-funded liberal. Historically, too, conservatives won so often that liberals marked their rare victories by referring, for example, to the "(James) Allred era" of the 1930's or to the "(Ralph) Yarborough era" of the 1950's.

The evolution of competition in Texas politics really began in 1961, when John G. Tower won a special U.S. Senate election to replace then-Vice President Lyndon Johnson. Tower, a former college economics professor, not only was the first Republican to win a statewide election since Reconstruction, but he defeated a conservative Democrat. Tower subsequently was re-elected and became a national Republican leader. But the GOP's actual Texas breakthrough came in 1978, when Republican oil-driller Bill Clements was elected governor and began systematically building both a party infrastructure and a farm team of political talent that concentrated on state, not just national, politics.

Clements also inaugurated the escalation of political fund-raising — in a broad sense. He was the first state official to have an immediate background for that, to begin with: Just six years before he ran for governor, he was the Texas finance director of the Committee to Re-Elect the President (the Richard Nixon CREEP campaign that, among other things, financed the tactics that led to the Watergate scandal). Also, his business background as head of his own international oil-drilling company and then his exposure to the defense industry as President Nixon's second-term deputy secretary of Defense, in addition to the political connections from the Republican National Committee tenure of his then-new wife Rita Bass Clements, gave Clements access to wealthy donors. More importantly, for the future of other GOP candidates, Clements instilled in Texas Republicans, many of whom previously only opened their checkbooks to presidential and U.S. Senate candidates, the idea that they must contribute to both state and local party candidates if they expected to make Texas a competitive two-party state.

It's true that Clements lost a bid for a second term as governor, as did the entire statewide executive-branch slate of 1982 Republicans. But they lost because a well-financed, coordinated Democratic campaign led by Sen. Lloyd Bentsen promoted a ticket that, for the first time, included conservatives, moderates and liberals. It also was the Democrats' last big hurrah, in that 1982 was the party's last executive-branch sweep. By contrast, the 1998 election 16 years later was the Republicans' first executive-branch sweep of state offices, which coincided with the first-ever election of all Republicans on the two statewide courts. And 1998 proved Republican hegemony in fund-raising, as all statewide and legislative GOP candidates raised $83 million to only $38 million for all Democrats. (Actually, that number was distorted by Gov. George W. Bush's vacuum cleaner of a campaign against under-funded Democrat Garry Mauro; but even with that race backed out, Republicans out-raised Democrats by $57 million to $33 million.)

★   ★   ★

The election culminating in 1998 also made clear how concentrated are the big givers in Texas politics. The sprawling Houston metropolitan area provided $15.1 million to statewide and legislative candidates, and more than half of that was from just five ZIP codes. The Austin-San Marcos metro area added $13.5 million, and more than half of that came from just the two ZIP codes where lobbyists and lobby groups mostly get and send their mail. The Dallas side of the Metroplex contributed $10.1 million, and $3.2 million of it came from two downtown ZIP codes. The Fort Worth side of the Metroplex added $2.6 million, of which nearly half was from just the big downtown ZIP code. San Antonio added $3.2 million, Beaumont-Port Arthur $1.3 million and Midland-Odessa just under $1 million.

The top sources of this statewide and legislative Texas campaign money, which also includes contributions to party committees, came from the usual suspects of interest groups and individuals — and in approximate proportion to their direct financial stake in state government. At the top of the list are lawyers and lobbyists with $13.1 million, followed by finance interests (banks, insurance, real estate), $12.1 million; energy and natural resources, $9 million; ideological or single-issue PACs, $8.5 million; miscellaneous business interests, $6.9 million; health care, $4.9 million; communications and electronics, $3.7 million; construction, $3.4 million; agriculture-related, $2.6 million; transportation, $2 million; labor, $1.5 million; and "other" interests, $2.3 million.

It might surprise some Texans to know that the biggest individual contributors in 1998 were businessmen contributing to their own campaigns — David Dewhurst, $3.2 million, who won his Republican campaign for land commissioner, and Paul Hobby, $2.9 million, who lost his Democratic campaign for comptroller. The other big hitters, all Republicans, were Houston homebuilder Bob Perry, $765,275; San Antonio businessman James Leininger, $456,784; Dallas entrepreneurs Charles and Sam Wyly, $406,500; Pittsburg poultry magnate Lonnie (Bo) Pilgrim, $388,349; and Houston businessman William A. McMinn, $380,500.

★   ★   ★

Among political action committees, the Republican Party of Texas ($2.2 million) and the Texas Democratic Party ($1.8 million) topped the charts, followed by Texans for Lawsuit Reform (tort reform), $1 million; the Houston-based Vinson & Elkins law firm, $635,753; the Texas Automobile Dealers Association, $632,149; Texas (Southwestern) Bell PAC, $594,129; the Texas Association of Realtors, $566,620; the Texas Medical Association, $506,793; the Texas Dental Association, $492,798; PSEL PAC (Bass family) of Fort Worth, $490,200; and the Houston-based Fulbright & Jaworski law firm PAC, $386,357.

Without picking on any interests per se, but looking for a non-trade-association PAC, let's take a more detailed look at PSEL PAC. It's an example of contributors who are political players with interests that are broader than just the Legislature or the governor's office. Start with the knowledge that Perry Bass and his sons are billionaires, whose original capital came from the Fort Worth-based Sid Richardson oil and gas fortune. Their business interests now span the national and international economies, so their interests aren't limited to an issue or two every couple of years before the Railroad Commission. They gave $117,000 to George W. Bush's re-election campaign; $55,000 to Rick Perry, now the Republican lieutenant governor, and $35,000 to Democrat John Sharp, who lost to Perry; $86,500 to John Cornyn, the Republican who was elected attorney general; $45,000 to Carole Keeton Rylander, the Republican elected comptroller, and $5,000 to losing Democrat Paul Hobby; $25,000 to GOP land commissioner winner David Dewhurst; $12,500 to GOP agriculture commissioner Susan Combs; and $22,500 to new Republican Railroad Commissioner Tony Garza. But their business interests sometimes end up in state courts, so they also contributed to incumbent Republican Supreme Court Justices Greg Abbott ($14,000) and Craig Enoch ($16,500), and to new Republican Justices Deborah Hankinson ($20,000) and Harriet O'Neill ($13,000).

★   ★   ★

The point is that economic interests that invest in Texas politics do so for a variety of reasons, and in a variety of campaigns. You can learn more about the motivations of givers and the feelings of the getters by reading the interviews with some of those who actually asked for and used contributions in legislative races. The interviews are in Chapter 7.

6

"If you're in office, if you're the incumbent, you are in a position where you've got to go back again and again for the money...But the process of asking...forces you to spend a lot of time with the people who give you money. And I think there is a human tendency...people like to say what other folks want to hear. That may just be my politician speaking."

— *From former Rep. Alec Rhodes, D–Dripping Springs, on the political communication of money*

★   ★   ★

Polls
↳ study of

POLLS AND POLITICAL HOLES

No one of sound mind, surely, would argue that public-opinion surveys alone should be allowed to dictate public policy. After all, in a representative democracy, we are supposed to elect some of our best and brightest fellow citizens to make independent decisions for the nation, the state, the county, the city, the school district, etc. Never mind, I guess, that fewer and fewer of us actually exercise our right to vote in the elections at which our more politically engaged brothers and sisters do the choosing of our public-policy proxies. At the same time, the average voter would probably be astounded at the extent to which surveys of public opinion, which most of us call polls, already dictate public policy — or at least dictate the policy that flows from campaign advertisements. Indeed, the average voter would be appalled that the so-called issues of a given well-financed campaign for public office at almost any level were largely framed in the first place by what political strategists, and through them the candidate, have learned from the polls.

This is not, however, a lecture on polls and their uses. If the American people were not already enchanted with the commercial results of public-opinion surveys, after all, we would still be using grocery-store-label baking soda to clean our teeth and lye soap to clean our bodies — much less, possibly, watching television programs of "cleaner" content. Rather, this chapter concentrates on a few sweeping generalizations about political polls and what we tell the pollsters compared to how we actually believe and behave, and on one particular poll that puts campaign finance in a special spotlight.

We constantly say that we prefer clean, issue-oriented campaigns for public office. Yet our voting behavior obviously is influenced, to a measurable degree, by what political operatives call "comparative" but we voters call "negative" advertising. It is demonstrably true that some winners of campaigns don't get nasty about their opponents and that sometimes issues do drive the results of some campaigns. But if it's a close race, the odds are good that one side or the other will perhaps not aim for the gutter, but at least skid near it. And if one side does so and the other has the financial means to respond, the odds are even better that a campaign gets down and dirty in a hurry. Assuming approximately equal resources on both sides, it's not even unreasonable to speculate that both sides had prepared in advance for such a turn south — by polling, ever so quietly, on messages that test the voter appeal of certain arguments or facts.

★   ★   ★

Again, as with other elements of this book, the amount of money available to a campaign has a great deal to do with its likely use. A financially strapped candidate isn't likely to squander money on polls about hypothetical negative questions about the opponent that might gain some ground. The financially flush candidate, on the other hand, can wisely anticipate the worst, and one possibility is a feeling that the campaign must at least be prepared to "go negative" (if, presumably, late-in-the-election polls indicate the value of doing so).

Even the clean, issue-oriented campaign may not be what it appears on the surface. A classic campaign tactic is to take a candidate's basic positions on four or five issues (not too many to overload or confuse us voters) and attach catchy names to the candidate's "plan" for those issues. The poll-driven part of the tactic, if a campaign can afford to do so, is to test the voters for the right phrases that create warm, fuzzy feelings in the voters' brains. Think of "a chicken in every pot" during a time of great hunger. And those phrases are adopted even if there's a big qualifier attached to each of the promises — for example, you have to pay for the pot somehow before you're entitled to stand in line for the chicken.

The most important thing is how the phrase connects with and persuades the voters, and the most definitive way to know that is to conduct polls. The candidate without the money to do that, and certainly the one without the money to plaster the catch-phrase plan on posters and signs and over the air waves, is reduced to explaining his own issues in complete sentences. Perhaps he can do that in campaign white papers that are only read by editorial writers and by those without anything else to do. And, what do we the voters do? Mostly we watch politics on TV — and not just the news, but talk shows and comedy as well.

What about when the winning candidate takes office, burdened as an incumbent only by the buzzwords he or she used in the campaign? Believe it or not, those poll-tested phrases often become the basis for legislation. And if, say, the poultry industry takes up the hypothetical "chicken in every pot" idea in the form of a real bill, the chicken people will do their own polling to see precisely what the people actually want (fryer vs. broiler, for example); and how they want it packaged (whole, half or in parts); as well as how they want it cooked (fried, boiled, broiled). That bill then will become part of the industry's legislative program, well-advertised, and might even help the industry avoid coverage of its simultaneous attempt to emasculate the federal regulation of chicken-killing.

We have seen earlier that the best-financed candidate wins the overwhelming percentage of campaigns, that an incumbent seeking re-election is an odds-on winner and that the certainty rises to the 95th percentile of probability if the incumbent is also the best-financed. Yet we the voters also tell pollsters that campaigns cost too much, and that big-money campaigns, particularly at the federal level, have a corrosive, even corruptive effect. Some polls in recent years have even reinforced the general perception that voters think "all politicians are crooked," but that is a more harsh judgement than most pollsters believe is true. (On the other hand, most pollsters work for a politician or two in their careers.) Political reporters generally agree that most politicians aren't themselves corrupt, but reporters, like pollsters, also want to claim the same kind of innocence asserted by the piano-player in the brothel.

*   *   *

But a single poll in June, 2000, and published July 28, which didn't get much publicity, yields a unique perspective on attitudes toward high-dollar politics. In a survey paid for by the left-leaning Institute for America's Future and The Nation magazine, the reputable but basically Democratic polling firm of Lake, Snell, Perry and Associates canvassed 1,000 voters and 200 contributors of at least $5,000 to national candidates since 1997 (100 from each major party). Among the poll's results:

• 52 percent of the voters and 41 percent of the contributors believe that "special interests and lobbyists" have the "most control over what goes on in Washington, D.C." — far more control than exercised by President Clinton and the Republican congressional leadership.

• Three-fourths of the voters and 53 percent of the contributors say business has too much influence in Washington; 44 percent of contributors say business influence is about right or is too little.

• Nearly three-fourths of both the voters and the contributors believe that members of Congress decide how to vote, half the time or more, based on what their contributors want, rather than on what they really believe.

• Seven out of 10 voters think that companies that lobby and give political contributions while getting government contracts are engaging in "legalized bribery"; 43 percent of the contributors agree, while 44 percent describe those companies as engaged in "a normal and ethical part of doing business."

Not surprisingly, on questions about specific issue areas — the use of the federal budget surplus, Social Security reform, international trade, etc. — the disagreements between voters and contributors were more clear-cut. But the point is, rather, that our attitudes toward big-money influence in politics have been measured and are consistent; this is simply the only poll that I know of that compares ordinary voters against high-dollar contributors. Moreover, the simple fact is that this poll underlines one theme of the book: Nobody would have thought those contributors worthy of polling, contrasted to voters in general, if they hadn't given a significant amount of money to politicians. Yet the contributors' attitudes aren't all that far out of line with those of voters in the survey, despite the contributors' being older, whiter, richer, and more male than the electorate in general.

7

"My position, when I first ran for public office,
was that I would take contributions from anybody,
except I would not knowingly take contributions from
the Mafia or the Communist Party of the United States."

*— From Bob Davis, former House member from Irving, former aide to Gov. Bill Clements
and former lobbyist who now practices law*

★   ★   ★

PERSPECTIVES
FROM SOME OF THE PLAYERS

A major goal of this book is to share with readers the attitudes toward campaign finance voiced by some former legislators, who have raised and spent money contributed by supporters and some of whom also have been on the contributing end as lobbyists. This is by no means a scientific sample, which would probably be impossible, anyway. Rather, former lawmakers were chosen because they offer unique perspectives on how and why campaign money is raised and whether, and if so how, they think the law should be changed. These interviews, conducted by former veteran Capitol reporter Anne Marie Kilday, appear almost in their entirety.

Transcript of interview with Don Adams, former Democratic House member and Senator from Jasper, now a lobbyist and lawyer.

Anne Marie Kilday: Quoting numbers from the last election: $121 million was spent, 55 percent of it in contributions of $1,000 or more, and more than half from fewer than 700 PACs and individuals. Do those numbers surprise you?

Adams: Yeah, they sure do. It doesn't surprise me about the PACs. There are still some huge PACs out there that take in a lot of money; but they are making substantial contributions—trial lawyers, as well as bankers, real estate and the automobile dealers — that's about the list. But it does surprise me, too, about the 700 individuals.

AMK: What does that say about the campaign system in Texas?
Adams: That there's about 700 people in Texas that have an enormous say in state government. I want to tell you, these people in public office now are just money-rais-

ing machines. You know, when I was in office, and that was well over 10 years ago, I never had a fundraiser; I never came to Austin to raise money. I'm not sure what caused the change. I got a call today from a House member—I am on somebody's list—I mean, they are just money-raising machines. I guess everybody in public office, or who aspires to be in public office, has that same list from Sam [Kinch]'s research. There is another PAC out there, too, which is the corporate or defense counsels. PACs, as you know, are substantially the creation of Common Cause — and what they were demanding was that you could have a place for employees to donate to, with accountability and all of that stuff. And now, they hate PACs. Yet what's really interesting to me, and has been over the years, is that who is giving money to whom, and how much, seems to be a lot more interesting to the press and the officeholders than it does to the public.

Former State Senator Don Adams:

"People think they are not in power, and the special interests are — and I think they are right."

AMK: When you look at [Arizona Sen.] John McCain's presidential candidacy, it does show some resonance with the public?

Adams: Not really. I think his candidacy was only part of that — I think part of it was about Democrats sending George Bush a message, and part of it was the whole thing of reform…[If it resonated with the public], we would have it. The Republicans up there in Congress are just stonewalling, and in the state Legislature, [Speaker] Pete Laney is the only one who even throws his hat at it; and it never gets anywhere. My point is — if people cared about it, it would go somewhere.

AMK: Is it a matter of people not knowing what they don't know? When you go to the Ethics Commission, doesn't even that require a special knowledge?

Adams: Probably, but the candidates know about it, and they try to make issues about it. I never thought, when I was voting on all that reform legislation in 1973…all of that disclosure stuff I thought was good, because the press would write about it. But, I never thought the average person would go out there [to read a campaign finance report]. I don't think you can design such a system.

AMK: Do you think people have the idea that government is bought and paid for by special interests?

Adams: Yes. I think that people have an ill-defined conception of what you just said. I don't think they have a sophisticated conception, or necessarily an informed conception of that. I do think that people think they are not in power, and the special interests are — and I think they are right.

AMK: Why do you say that?

Adams: Because I think, essentially, the average citizen is not in power in government. Even when I was in office, and in the Congress, too...the only time you ever see the general public really paid attention to is when something happens that is really [a result of] people coming together. Sharpstown [the banking and stock-fraud scandal in 1971-72] was one of those things. Sharpstown was so ugly, so blatant, and so nasty, that the public demanded something be done. Something was done...and they [the voters] were satisfied, and they went away. I don't mean to be cynical, but I've thought a lot about this.

AMK: Why are the candidates today money machines? Is it because of the cost of campaigning?

Adams: They have to be. When I ran for office I wrote all my own ads for radio; I had no television, and I didn't have a campaign manager, except for myself. I think the advent of all of these political consultants, all of this sophisticated campaigning, phone banks, and all of that kind of stuff — principally, political consultants — have driven the cost of this stuff up. They know the things that you [need to] do that work, and it all costs a lot of money. And to be in the race, you've got to have a campaign manager that knows how to do all of that stuff. It's not like when I ran, when you could get out and walk door-to-door shaking hands. And [former Texas House member and Senator, later Congressman] Charlie Wilson and I ran the same way — we walked door-to-door handing out cards, bought newspaper and radio ads — and it elected us. The guy I ran against spent $65,000, and I spent $15,000 and beat him. That day has come and gone, because the minute one of you gets a campaign manager that knows how to use computers, and knows how to do phone banks, knows how to do direct mail, then the other side has got to do the same thing. And, all of those things are extremely expensive. Also, in some of the legislative races, and virtually all of the statewide races, you really have got to have television, and that has just run up the cost of campaigning. The system is just driving itself now.

AMK: What impact does money have? Does it have more impact on legislative outcomes? Does it buy access?

Adams: No question about it, it buys access.

AMK: Does it buy government?

Adams: I don't think so; it's a complex answer to that question. I really think that, by and large, most of the people in the Legislature try to do the right thing...they probably are better than when I was there. But, they are human beings and when they see the Texas Medical Association, or when they see Dick Weekley [through the Texans for Lawsuit Reform PAC] give Wayne Christian $65,000 to win a House seat that I spent $15,000 to win...even factoring in inflation, it's obscene. I'm not trying to be personal; I'm just using that example. Given that, they [legislators] look at it and they say, 'I think I'll try to figure out a way that this is good public policy.' And so, I think it's a complex set of hoops they jump through to sort of get to...'They haven't bought government; they've just scared it into doing what they want it to do.' That's sort of a Jasper way of saying it, I guess.

AMK: When you look back at the 'bad old days,' did the lobby have more control? Or was it just a 'good old boy system?'

Adams: It was both. It was both, and I'll tell you a story. When I was a freshman House member, I spent most of my time in [former Lt. Gov.] Ben Ramsey's office trying to figure things out, learning from him. I didn't spend much time around other legislators. We had a special session — and I didn't know who the hell Harry Whitworth [then chief executive of the Texas Chemical Council] was. [Gov.] Preston Smith called a special session, and he proposed a chemical tax. Well, I want you to know that a lot of people got to know who Harry Whitworth was. Harry couldn't go to the speaker, [because] the governor had put it in the call, he had put it on the table. It was something that had to be considered. Harry Whitworth had to go around and talk to people like me about the chemical companies. Before Sharpstown, there was a lot of special interest business, a lot of lobby business, that went on in the speaker's office, and in the committee chairmen's offices. And I think Preston Smith kind of uncovered that in that session. Sharpstown kind of opened up the political process, where if you had a problem you could just go down to the speaker's office and have it taken care of, or to the governor's office. I'm sure some of that is done now, but not nearly like it was.

AMK: Do you think the Ethics Commission we have now is effective?
Adams: No. Who has been prosecuted?

AMK: Nobody. Nobody formally.
Adams: I was treasurer of a PAC and I got fined $100 [for a late report]. Big deal. It's like highway patrolmen giving speeding tickets to people out there killing folks.

★　　★　　★

Transcript of interview with Bill Clayton, former Democratic House member from Springlake and former House speaker, now an Austin lobbyist.

Anne Marie Kilday: Is there a need to clean up Texas' campaign finance law?

Clayton: I've got the best proposal to clean up campaign finance in the world, if I could only find somebody with the balls to run with it; but I don't think any of them would do it.

AMK: Why is it necessary?

Clayton: The reason I think it is necessary is I think we need to do something where everybody who wants to seek office at least feels like they have a chance, a fighting chance; and that the general public doesn't think they have to buy their way into an office. And that would, I think, take the apathy out of the voters and make them feel like they could make a difference.

AMK: What would your proposal do about it?

Clayton: I have proposed [contribution] limits, but that's not the only thing. If you give $100 to a candidate running for office and somebody else gives $50,000, who's going to have that open door policy a little better?

AMK: You tell me; you were there.

Clayton: I can tell you two or three things. I can tell you that I did not know who contributed to me, and that was unique. I'm not saying that [former chief of staff] Jack Gullahorn probably didn't know, or [also former chief of staff] Rusty Kelley; but I didn't keep up with that. I do know that some candidates do, because I've witnessed it.

AMK: How big a role does money play down there?

Clayton: Well, I don't think money buys anything [concrete], but it does [buy] access; it puts you in position [when you want] appointments. But I don't think you can buy votes. I've only seen that occur one time in my life here in Austin.

Former Speaker Billy Clayton:

**"I think we need to do something where everybody
who wants to seek office at least feels like they have a chance,
a fighting chance; and that the general public doesn't think
they have to buy their way into an office.
And that would, I think, take the apathy out of the voters
and make them feel like they could make a difference."**

AMK: And when was that?

Clayton: That was a long time ago, when I saw a senator sell a vote. Now I've had a lot of members tell me they were going to do something and then do something else. It was just a matter of who got to them last. They lied. You know, I've heard politicians do that. But the access really is important. I think everybody ought to have equal access to their politicians, and thataway they'd feel like they had a greater say-so. I think there'd be less apathy in the electoral process; I think it's sad that we don't have more participating in the electoral process.

AMK: People just don't vote.

Clayton: I think it's a big reason. When I first ran for the Legislature in 1962, I had two primary opponents, and they were pretty tough opponents. I had one general election opponent. So I ran the primary race. One of the guys was the editor of the newspaper in Dimmitt, Texas. I won that run-off and the general election. That cost me $6,000.

AMK: When you became speaker, it was different?

Clayton: Oh, yes. It was different because I hardly had any opposition out there, hopefully because I did a good job. It might be they just didn't know me. But when you become speaker, your visibility is higher, and then you have opponents recruited to run against you. Now, of course, it's getting worse, because when I was elected we didn't have a single Republican in the House. You were either a conservative Democrat or a liberal Democrat. It was a one-party state. Now, I know the parties have made the competition in races higher, but golly, [the cost of] some of these races...ridiculous!

AMK: I know you came up with some reforms as speaker, and then there were more reforms in '91.

Clayton: There's a step further we should have gone. I don't believe you should have officeholder accounts. If you are in office and you are performing a duty you should be performing, the state should pay for it. The taxpayers shouldn't be called on to buy you extra staff and extra mailers [to constituents] and things like that. If you want to send extra mailers, the taxpayers shouldn't pay for it. Back before we limited the use of those accounts, we actually had people buy cars and homes and those kinds of things. Buying a house isn't what campaign money is for.

AMK: You also made big Speaker's Day changes.

Clayton: Oh yes, gifts were just lavished on the speaker. I can remember, for example, when we bought Byron Tunnel a new Pontiac on Speaker's Day. It was brand spanking new. He was just one example. Everybody was done that way, so I decided to change it, to make contributions to Girlstown and Boys Ranch USA. It seemed like we split about $20,000 between the two each year.

AMK: When you left office, where did your officeholder account go?

Clayton: I donated to A&M and part of it to Girlstown and Boys Ranch USA. But voters aren't contributing for those purposes. In reality, I would like to see big, big contributions done away with, but if we don't do that, we ought to do away with letting people accumulate funds for [later] campaigns. Once an election is over, they should have to balance out and do something with those funds, not have any carryover. If they have debt, that's just tough luck; they didn't plan right. And thataway, you'd give people out there — who are not incumbents — a feeling that they might have a shot at this [election success].

AMK: You and Clayton Williams were good friends, but how much did he spend running for governor [as a Republican] in 1990?

Clayton: Eight million bucks — of his own money. And, I'm kind of the one who talked him into running. We were hunting [later] out on a ranch he had leased, and he said, 'Goddamnit, if I hadn't run for governor, I could own this ranch.'

AMK: Was he sorry?

Clayton: In a lot of ways, he was; in others, he wasn't. In my opinion, a good campaign manager could've prevented that.

AMK: What about putting that much money in your own campaign?

Clayton: Well, look at [Republican Land Commissioner David] Dewhurst [who spent $3.2 million of his own money]. In all honesty, I don't have that much trouble with people putting their own money into it. Maybe that makes them get out there and hustle and try to win. But, it's a gamble and you know it going in. If you've got the money, it's your privilege, but it does limit people without money from going in. So my reform program would also provide for a certain amount of access to the airwaves that are licensed for public use in campaigns allotted to candidates—and not 30-second spots. Something to get the issues out and let people know who the people are they are going to be voting for — both the electronic media and the print. I think it's a public service to let people know who is running for election. I don't know what form it would take; those details could be worked out.

AMK: You don't think [legislators] have the nerve? It's kind of catching on nationally.

Clayton: I think it would be a popular thing with the public, and a resented thing among the members. So, you have to figure out what to do when the members go: 'Oh well, that son of a bitch, why did he introduce that?' They know if it gets laid out, they have to vote for it. So, even if it does get introduced, they'd try to kill it in committee.

AMK: What about PACs? Should they be done away with?

Clayton: They should allow corporations and labor unions to contribute, and let the people know about it, instead of hiding behind PACs. I just don't think the general public can figure it out, and there's where you'd have to have your limits. I think the key is disclosure. If you begin to see a certain group of people contribute to a candidate and it makes you feel kind of queasy, then it will make you think a second or third time about that candidate. People are not going to give their money to people who are not going to support their issues. [But now] people don't know. Or, they are misled.

AMK: What about these new [hard to identify] groups running legislative ads?
Clayton: Well, they are just deceptive. They ought to be required to tell who's running those ads.

★   ★   ★

Transcript of interview with Bob Davis of Irving, a former Republican House member, former aide to Gov. Bill Clements, and former lobbyist, who is now practicing law.

Anne Marie Kilday: Campaign finance seems to be catching on with, particularly, some people in your party.

Davis: It seems to be, particularly [Republican presidential candidate John] McCain went a long way with that issue.

AMK: And it also seems to be that some people here in Texas are going to be pushing it.

Davis: I wouldn't be surprised.

AMK: [Sam] Kinch and I are interviewing people who were around during the changes that were made with the creation of the Ethics Commission, and [and former Speaker Bill] Clayton's own efforts to limit uses of campaign funds. Do you feel there's a need for reform in Texas?

Davis: I sometimes have doubts about the efficaciousness of all of these efforts and I have kind of put it in perspective. Well, my perception is that [reformers] have a perception that somebody is getting a better shake out of the system; and they are getting a better shake because of the way they participate in elections. And they would choose not to participate in the elections themselves, and so they don't. What they attempt to do is limit somebody else's participation in elections. I am of the opinion that there has been no single more important factor in the growth of the Republican Caucus than what is commonly called income. Right after that, you start having friends that you've known for a long time who have very deep pockets, both as to their wisdom and to their friendship. Those people tend to be much more persuasive in the process than political contributions, but it's the political contributions that tend to gain the notoriety.... [Davis quoted British parliamentarian Benjamin Disraeli: 'Reform is often the cloak under which a greater evil advances.'] I think a lot of reform is like that. Soft money wasn't an issue until the federal government went through their advances; and suddenly soft money became more insidious than hard money, because it was harder to track. I noticed somebody in the paper the other day saying, 'Texas law makes it hard to track because you don't have to put down where you work, [and] you're not giving us all the information that you can about donors.'

Former Rep. Bob Davis:

"The truth is, I think most politicians are aware who their contributors are. Gracious me, they certainly would tell their contributors that."

AMK: Well, don't you think people need to know that? What if they are trial lawyers? Should they say that?

Davis: Don't you think the process points that out, anyway? Here's my thinking on this: If the public needs to know, then you have to have a communications source. The public is not going to know if it's just in the abstract, and so the communications aspect most people assign either to the opposition campaign or the press. Sometimes, the press' position, as you know, is — 'It's up to the opposition to bring it up. We're not going to write about it if somebody doesn't say something about it.' Sometimes, the [press] viewpoint is that — 'It's our duty to write about issues, whether a candidate talks about it or not.' So I say, 'Wait a minute, are we really talking about making somebody's job easier? Are we talking about the information being put forward so the people who are going to do the communicating can get to it quicker?'

AMK: What's wrong with that?

Davis: I'm not saying there's anything wrong with that. I'm just saying should it be a function of government to put this type information in a way so a reporter who wants to do the story doesn't have to go get the information. Is it a relevant issue to campaigns? Sure. My position, when I first ran for public office, was that I would take contributions from anybody, except I would not knowingly take contributions from the Mafia or the Communist Party of the United States. It frankly didn't make any difference to me whether it [the contribution report] included the employment history of a person or not. If a candidate is taking trial lawyer money or big business money, it's going to be public information.

AMK: Let's move beyond the campaign, into the legislature. Does [campaign money] affect legislation?

Davis: Sure. I read all the stories. But nobody bought anything by contributing.

AMK: You really believe that to be true?

Davis: On the surface, that probably is an accurate statement, in terms of being able to compel somebody to make a decision one way or another. But, for so many issues in the Legislature, the Congress or the body politic, it's strictly — them versus us. The man in expensive clothing just doesn't have a dog in the hunt at all. It's one segment of society trying to band together to catch up with another segment of society.

AMK: But does money buy access?

Davis: Sure. The truth is, I think most politicians are aware who their contributors are. Gracious me, they certainly would tell their contributors that.

AMK: Don't you write thank-you notes?

Davis: Well, I always did, and the first thing that was said to me was, 'You should never forget that people and money are the mother's milk of politics.' And, when push comes to shove, that's really the ultimate code to victory. Does it matter how somebody comes to the right decision? The bottom line being that you're not going to produce a different result.

AMK: The Ethics Commission just went on-line. Should there be some real valid way of identifying [contributors], I mean, like to the Good Roads Association?

Davis: I tend to think that is not particularly important in the long term. Again, is it relevant to the issues of a campaign? And if it is relevant, the information gets out there.

AMK: Does [raising] money prevent good people from entering politics?

Davis: I suspect that money, time and abuse from the public all play significant roles in keeping people out. We're having this discussion about money being so bad, and if money is so bad, why can't these people get it?

AMK: You didn't mind calling people for money?
Davis: I hated it. I hated it, but I got over it. There are a lot of people who would like to contribute, if you just ask them. I think that's one reason that political action committees took off. I think the focus at first was trying to be together — a political connection.

AMK: Was there ever any issue, when you were in the House, when money made the difference [in a vote]?
Davis: I'm trying to think. Yeah. Once upon a time, a fight was going on between the insurance agents and the bankers over the ability of banks and savings and loans to sell insurance. Durward Curlee [savings and loan lobbyist] stopped me at one point and said, 'Hey, at some point we may need your help on this.' And I looked at him and said, 'Curlee, I'm chairman of the Insurance Committee and the insurance [lobbyists] have been my friends ever since I've been running for public office, and the savings and loan people that I know kind of came later. These people are my friends, they've contributed to me and supported me every time I've run, and so you're too late on this issue.' And, so I think that one…uh…I don't know that, that was exclusively money in that sense; but it was an issue that I already had taken a position on back a long time ago, and I wasn't going to change it. But it was one where I knew I had received considerable contributions from the insurance guys.

★   ★   ★

Transcript of interview with Robert Earley, a former Democratic House member from Portland, who lost a race for the Railroad Commission and is now a college professor of ethics and government.

Anne Marie Kilday: Does the campaign finance law need to be changed?

Earley: I would take one step backward and say it's real-ly the incredible control that you have with the lobby structure and the money that you give, when you pay legislators $600 per month. We, as Texans, think that's wonderful. I know that when I got into office at age 23, 24, I didn't have any money. I had none. And, having the luxury of those guys [lobbyists] taking me to lunch and dinner was fantastic, because I couldn't have financially made it. Is that an indictment on me, or is that survival trying to be a representative? I, of course, would argue with anybody...that, that wasn't a great deal of influence. My God, that's a hell of an open door, and that's not something that you're going to say, 'Well, I'm not going to have dinner with the lobbyists.' Well, with the atmosphere we have in Texas...that sort of isolates you. Secondly, it was critical, because my $375 check a month [take-home pay] didn't go very far. So, we just tend to let the system break down totally by this misconception that if we pay legislators less and we have them all part-time, that we'll have this citizen-type legislator — we're not going to pay those bums, they're making money on the side, anyway. Well, the sure-fire way to do it is to get guys in here and women in here who can't afford it; so, you start a concrete business. You start crap like that — it makes deals and you make money.

AMK: What about the issue of big money? When you look at the last statewide and legislative campaigns that cost $121 million...and it was collected from fewer than 700 people and PACs — is that healthy?

Earley: No, it's not healthy, and I can report on that on a personal level. And, it's not bragging on our campaign against [then-incumbent Democratic Railroad Commissioner] Jim Nugent, but that's a classic case of a guy with no money [running against] a guy with a lot of money. First of all, you can say Nugent had name identi-fication, but that's not true because nobody in Texas has name identification of any size. I don't care who you are — unless you are Ann Richards or George Bush. Our campaign met with 21 [newspaper] editorial boards; we picked up 18 endorsements. It didn't make any difference, none at all. It all was a money race. Anywhere we went, the responses were good. From the Democratic clubs, we got significant endorsements. All the machinery of politics went to us, except for money. My numbers tracked just about like anybody who runs against a well-financed incumbent. You are going to get about 32 percent of the vote. If you do really well, you'll get about 39 percent. We probably spent, all in all, I can't even remember, but we were up around $200,000 to $250,000; and Nugent spent about $825,000. In El Paso and Houston and all, it's just a slam-dunk [for Nugent]. In just about any other state I could have easily gotten elected. Well, I shouldn't say have easily gotten elected — we could have run a neck-and-neck race. In Texas, where you've got Dallas, Houston and West Texas media [to finance], when your race only boils down to media, it just lends itself to the big boys having a bigger voice.

AMK: So you think it's media-driven?

Earley: I think it is in Texas. That's where you have to spend your money. I'm talking television. When you can drop $50,000, $60,000 on TV in the Houston market, you can do something. We had, I think the last week of the election, we were going to be seen by 2 out of 10 viewers watching television. Nugent was going to be up for four weeks and was going to hit 6 of 10 of the viewers. It didn't matter how many endorsements you had out there, or how much support you had from the real, true politicos, if you got beat on the television ads. From a television standpoint, in modern times, I think it's significant...I mean, look at David Dewhurst and Richard Raymond [in another financial mismatch for land commissioner in 1998].... There are anomalies along the way. If you get a Reagan Brown [the Democratic agriculture commissioner in 1982] who talks [degradingly] about George Washington Carver, that's an anomaly or Jim Hightower [who defeated Brown in that year's primary] would never have started his career.

AMK: Is it more, also, that politics is now a commercial enterprise driven by pollsters and not posters? That you have to have consultants and those things?

Earley: I don't know. It's a hard question. You do have to have the whole [campaign package] thing. You could have cases where they didn't have that. I think that doing business in Texas from a political standpoint, it's so incredibly costly because it is so big; you can't campaign in all those markets. If I had it to do again, I wouldn't have gone to Houston other than to have fundraisers. We had a schedule that last week, where I did puddle jumpers and made six stops a day. People would say, 'Goddamn, that guy can speak and he is incredibly funny.' I'd leave there on a high. If I'd gone into Longview and raised $10,000, I would have made significantly more impact.

AMK: How did you feel about asking for money?

Earley: Oh, I hated it. The two hardest things I've done in my brief political career was when I was 23, and going up and knocking on a door and saying, 'Hi, I'm Robert Earley and would you vote for me?' I thought that was the hardest thing to do. Until in a statewide campaign, I had to go to someone I had never even met and ask them for money. It was gut-wrenching. I hated it. I hated it. The worst story I had was I called one gentleman, who was a big Democratic-giver, and he said, 'Mr. Earley, I've heard your name and I know you were a House member. I have great respect for you.' And he said, 'I have cancer and I'm not even going to make it through this election.' I was given phone lists; and I would get on the phone every day, and [aides] would say, 'Call these 15 names.' And, guys like [then-Dallas now-Austin lawyer-lobbyist] Sandy Kress, who knew why I was calling, they never returned my phone calls…. Or that guy in Waco, [Democratic financier] Bernard Rapoport, who sat down and said, 'I like you. You've got guts, kid. I like you. Let me tell you, if you can just get Mike Millsap to say…because Mike's my guy at UT and if Mike says you're the man, I'm going to give you money.' And I jumped through that hoop. I had Mike call him, and I never heard from Rapoport again. Gosh, my old buddy over at the LCRA, who's now with Public Strategies, Mark Rose, I call him and he says, 'I'll meet with you in San Antonio and I've got a partner in Arizona and he'll give you money.' I never got any money. That's what tough is: You prostitute yourself asking for money and these people tell you the proverbial check is in the mail. And you had to do that. You hated it, you didn't like raising money, it was horrible. And as soon as it came in, it was gone. We pretty much ran a staff of pure volunteers. A lot of my students from St. Edwards. And [then-Comptroller] John Sharp loaned me a few of his [political] people.

Former Rep. Robert Earley:

"So, sure, there were times when members of the Texas Legislature would come up to me on the House floor and say, 'Don't you know who you are screwing on that vote?', and it never was, 'You're screwing voters,' it was 'You're screwing a money man.' And it changed votes."

AMK: Do you think that money…does it follow that money increases voter apathy? Is that a logical question?

Earley: It's a logical question; but we've always had voter apathy and I don't know why. Last semester, I talked a lot [in class] about how all the barriers to voting are being broken down and yet voters are voting less and less. And I don't know if it's the influence of money, or what the situation is. The soapbox selling of the candidates of today isn't all that different, it's just that we use a different medium to do it. And the campaigns…I don't think they are any nastier today. I don't think it's necessarily money. I do know the influence of getting people elected. But, the two causal links I can't draw: Does that situation mean apathy, or does that money mean that individual votes differently or not? I don't know, because a lot of folks once in office become cavalier…. I know that Harry Whitworth [the late chief executive] of the Texas Chemical Council helped me when I first got elected, and later sent a message that I wasn't doing very well for him once I was in office. And I sent a message back that I couldn't care less. I found that to be kind of bold and brazen. Shit, I was going to do what I wanted.

A connection between money and policy, though…it certainly looks like it at the presidential level. I could make a lot of arguments that Clinton and his friends have significantly influenced policies for China and a lot of other things. But, from the Texas Legislature I don't know. Now I could look at a guy like…Hugo Berlanga and say: 'You bet Hugo wasn't going to do anything to hurt his beer distributor buddy Harry Andrews in Corpus Christi, and he got all of his [campaign] money from guys like that.' I don't know that I'm helpful to you on that.

AMK: So there are instances where campaign contributions lead to votes?

Earley: Oh, sure. I remember voting on whether we ought to have air boats outside Galveston Island and somebody coming up to me saying, 'You just pissed off one of the Bass brothers.' I said, 'Does he live there?' And the member said, 'He's the guy with the money behind this thing. You need to back off.' To me, that was sort of the other side of the Robert Earley that says: 'Great, I'm going to make sure I vote to screw the Bass brothers.' I always felt like I had two sides, the side to go along and say, 'I'll go along to be on the Gib Lewis and the Pete Laney team' and then this other side that said, 'Screw you, I'm not doing that.' So, sure, there were times when members of the Texas Legislature would come up to me on the House floor and say, 'Don't you know who you are screwing on that vote?', and it never was, 'You're screwing voters,' it was 'You're screwing a money man.' And it changed votes. Those kinds of things happened. I'm giving you anecdotal evidence here, of course; I wouldn't know how to go about proving empirically that money changed votes.

AMK: What about campaign finance limits?

Earley: I've always supported it and I've never agreed with the argument that it violates the First Amendment. I've never bought the First Amendment argument that it suppresses freedom of speech. I've always thought if there were a European-style election, where you had less time to campaign, and you had individual amounts that a person would cap out at. [Critics] have always said that favors the incumbent, but I don't buy that…right now an incumbent has no caps. Take Nugent: If I could [have] capped him at $500,000, the argument that Earley never could have raised that… for every dime I got, Nugent would call those people and do a shake-down and get money from them. British Petroleum gave me $5,000 and Nugent called them and pissed on their leg, and they gave him $10,000. If you had a cap, it would stop incumbent spending, so [the challenger] would be half-reachable to their dollar amounts.

AMK: And, they have caps at the federal level.

Earley: Right. I think it would be the greatest thing ever. And it would be a significant help in Texas politics. Most of the need for money in Texas is significant. You can't campaign statewide [just] being a good candidate. If you are a good candidate, with good issues and hot issues, and a good campaign, it doesn't matter. It doesn't make any difference — I can cite numerous cases throughout history where it doesn't matter. You've got to have money here — buy media in Houston, buy it in LA, it's about the same cost.

AMK: What about requiring media to donate time?
Earley: I don't know. That's an avenue, but it's not a significant avenue. And, if you are being bombarded.... And also, debates are horrible, because you already have a person you like.... And if you require donated media, you're going to turn it off real quick. The only way that would work is if you had limited campaign time, which is real draconian for the United States.

AMK: Did you always know who your contributors were?
Earley: No, I did not. When I would have a fundraiser, you'd have 30 people show up. I never was concerned with who was there; I was concerned with 'did we hit our $40,000 goal?' That was always a dollar amount. The other thing I never really knew, which was about the only thing I got raked over the coals for, was when I had the fricking faux pas when I went to the Cher concert with the likes of [then-Sen.] John Montford and [House Speaker] Pete Laney. I never knew who the lobbyists [who paid for it] represented. When [Stan] Schlueter would come into the office, or Buddy Jones, or Rusty Kelley, I never knew who all their clients were. I didn't care. I knew who they were representing when they came into the office. And, the only money I ever returned was to the pari-mutuel horseracing folks, because they gave me too much when I was running. They gave me $1,000, and then they gave me $5,000. I said, 'Thanks, but no thanks.' I thought that somebody could easily make the argument that I was being influenced. I felt that I wasn't being influenced. I was going to vote for pari-mutuel horseracing whether they gave me money or not — it didn't make any difference. However, they were making it look like it had an influence. The only other money I returned, which I found out after I left office that most of my colleagues never did, was honoraria which people would give you when you'd go speak to their groups. I was amazed; I never knew that. I was naive on that. I learned who the Nelsons were [he remembers a time when someone older referred to 'Ozzie and Harriet' and Earley didn't know who the 1950s sit-com characters were], and I also

learned that people would get $750 to go and speak. I was amazed at that. I always gave that back. I remember speaking to the State Troopers Association and they gave me a $500 check. And I said I speak for free, it's my job.

AMK: What was their reaction?

Earley: I pissed them off. I remember [state troopers lobbyist, at the time] Lane Denton coming up and saying, 'You really screwed yourself here.' He said there were four other people [legislators] there who took the money. I spoke to colleagues and decided that if groups insisted on giving the money, which two of them did, I told them to put it in student scholarship funds; but it was not in my name. Of course, that was before the last round of ethics changes. It was real easy for me, but I just didn't do it [speak for money].

AMK: What's the best part of your teaching?

Earley: It's the challenge of knowing that 90 percent of your class has a cynical attitude and doesn't believe in the system. And, it's that challenge to say, 'No, it's a pretty good system.' Every three weeks we will have an ethics issue, and it will be something I will use from when I was in office. Like the guy back in my constituency, back in Sinton, Texas, every time he shook my hand there would be $500 in it. And, when I bought a house in Portland on foreclosure, I had a truck drive up with furniture in it from Lack's Furniture. And I said, 'Ya'll got the wrong house.' And they said, 'No, Mr. Kelly sent it. Are you Robert Earley?' He had bought furniture for my house. I said, 'Take it back.' And I remember, the day after I got elected a bunch of guys, who gave money to [former legislator, now lobbyist] Hugo Berlanga, delivered a car to my house. I sent that back immediately. I sent all that stuff back. It wasn't hard, it was easy. Part of it was easy because I was so damn poor, and I wasn't impressing any women.

AMK: You are kidding...a car was delivered? Now this man from Sinton, would you give him the money back?

Earley: Well, yeah, I gave it back every time. Finally, he got very frustrated with me, and I'm not sure he then voted for me the last couple of elections. He did it about three times and I gave it back every time. I told him I couldn't take it, that it was illegal, and he would laugh and do it again. And finally, I had to say, 'Stop doing this. I don't want it and I will never take it.' He never did it again, and he never seemed to want to sit around and joke with me and talk. Those kinds of things happened to me, and I tell my students about it. I say: 'What do you do? Nobody will know whether you took it or not. It's not reported.' And, I've been amazed. I've had students say, 'Yeah, take it.' Students say, 'Who would know? What does it matter?' In my campaign class, I talk about having terrible information on an opponent, [but] do you use it, knowing it might not be true? I've got students who say, 'Yeah, do it and deal with the ramifications later, because hopefully the ramifications will be later.' So, that's why you try to emphasize ethics in a positive way, as opposed to walking a holy path, you have to reason it through. If you realize they are that politically hungry, you have to talk about the ramifications of becoming [former Atty. Gen.] Jim Mattox and having the whole world out to get you. Or whatever.

★   ★   ★

Transcript of interview with Charles Gandy, former Democratic House member from Dallas, now an Austin-based municipal consultant who recently lost a Democratic U.S. Senate primary run-off.

Anne Marie Kilday: Given the numbers on the most recent statewide and legislative elections, what does this say about the Texas campaign finance system?

Gandy: Well, it says one dollar means one vote in Texas, or that corporations and their lobbyists are buying public policy in Texas. They arrange their army of lobbyists to make contributions in elections in Texas, and they expect votes to go their way.

AMK: So are you telling me they are buying public policy?

Gandy: Well, yes. I don't know of any corporation in Texas that has lobbyists in Austin who are there because of civic responsibility. Unfortunately, corporations are discovering that the political process is a battleground for profits.

AMK: Why are citizens turning away? Does it follow that they don't feel like they have a voice?

Gandy: Definitely. Cynicism.

AMK: What would you do to reform the Texas system?

Gandy: I have a proposal that I have presented to the House Elections Committee, which would require that the parties hold conventions to select statewide candidates by elections of the precinct chairs. [Note: State conventions would not, however, nominate legislative candidates.]

AMK: Playing devil's advocate, this sounds like returning to the smoke-filled rooms of days gone by.

Gandy: It's true, that is a risk, but it's really a matter of turning the elections over to the grass-roots activists who are active in the political process. And, we would bene-fit from having knowledgeable activists, so we don't get candidates like Gene Kelly [a Democrat who had run for a dozen public offices without success, but who beat Gandy in the 2000 Senate primary]. Both parties might draw better candidates.

Former Rep. Charles Gandy:

"Well, it says one dollar means one vote in Texas, or that corporations and their lobbyists are buying public policy in Texas. They arrange their army of lobbyists to make contributions in elections in Texas, and they expect votes to go their way."

AMK: That brings me to the next question. Is legislation for sale in Texas?
Gandy: Of course it is. Now not absolutely, but they are batting 800. I would bet that 8 out of 10 who contribute to candidates for public officeholders see the votes go their way.

AMK: What about adopting the federal contribution limit of $1,000?
Gandy: I would be for that.

AMK: Requiring media to donate time?
Gandy: I think that would go a long way. I'm in favor of free air time. I also tend to think that shows like "Hardball," which have an edge and stimulating conversation, do draw an audience [on cable TV]. That doesn't work for some people, however. [Former Agriculture Commissioner] Jim Hightower, for instance, tends to freeze up on that kind of show.

★   ★   ★

Transcript of interview with Bruce Gibson, former Democratic House member from Godley, former chief of staff to the late Lt. Gov. Bob Bullock, and now an executive with Reliant Energy of Houston (corporate parent of Houston Lighting and Power).

Anne Marie Kilday: What do the [contribution and expenditure] numbers say about Texas politics, and what, if anything, needs to be done?

Gibson: I can't honestly hear those numbers and look at those members, and say that money dictated a vote. I can't say it is distorting our system; I don't think it is distorting the system.

AMK: Does it prevent people from entering politics?
Gibson: I think that's more true on the federal level.

AMK: What's driving the campaign finance system? Is it the cost of campaigning?
Gibson: Campaign techniques are getting better and better, and it just costs more money to reach voters. TV costs more, and does less. So, the campaign consultants are just getting very clever. There are very clever ways of targeting demographic groups. We used to just think it was 'seniors.' Now, they cut it so many ways it's [down to] targeting senior Hispanics.

AMK: Let's talk about that role of consultants in your political life.
Gibson: When I first ran, I did not have a campaign consultant. It was very much a family-and-friend activity. We had a little brochure, and the total cost was $33,000. That was in 1980, 20 years ago. The character [of the campaign] was we didn't need any consultants, and there wasn't any money for polls. Now they do focus groups and consultants. The last race that I ran, in 1992, I did have a general consultant, and I spent $125,000. That was considered a very healthy campaign at the time. Today, members have to spend $300,000 to $400,000. One of the problems with restricting campaign contributions is that the costs of campaigns never go down, so the candidates borrow more money, or they have to put money in themselves.

AMK: Did the ethics reform changes lead to shifting the emphasis from trips and dinners to campaign checks?

Gibson: I think that clearly happened. I think there is definitely less emphasis on building [lobby] relationships [with legislators] through entertaining, and a lot more emphasis on building relationships through campaign contributions. Now, one thing is that we have not had a major ethics scandal since then. So, that may be a result of the ethics law, but I think it's also the cost of each campaign. We passed that bill in 1991, and 1992 was my last race, but costs of campaigns have tripled. And, we're talking this year about seeing a Texas Senate race where the candidates will spend $3 million. There are a lot of states in the United States where that's the cost of a campaign for the United States Senate. So, I think it's correct that ethics reform had some influence, but it's also the costs of campaigning. We [Reliant Energy] have one of the larger PACs in the state, and we really have a hard time stretching our budget. I'd say we're in the top five among corporate PACs, which is different from the trade association PACs.

AMK: Have you ever had members turn down money? Some members said they did, in the session before telephone deregulation.

Gibson: No. We're not receiving that complaint.

AMK: Do you think people feel like they are left out? Are voters aware of it?

Gibson: If you took everybody who gave that $121 million, that's just one or two percent [of the state's population]. Most of the public is completely disconnected from fundraising. Even though members go after that $1,000 or $5,000 contribution, there is still great emphasis and value put on those $25 contributions because they demonstrate popular support. They also energize people to get out and tell your story to their friends and put up signs and vote on Election Day, and to be part of your effort. I don't think the small contribution is unimportant at all, although most people are not convinced of that. The thought used to be that you wanted to have half your contributions coming in small contributions from your district. Now, I don't think anybody can do that any more.

AMK: Which brings us to that statistic about 80 percent of the money coming from outside the [average incumbent] lawmaker's district.

Gibson: Well, except for the member who represents downtown Austin, that is where the money comes from.

Former Rep. Bruce Gibson:

"I think you generally know who they [contributors] are, you are generally aware of who helped you. Some members will say they don't, but most members are generally aware."

AMK: That Austin Club schedule [for legislative candidates' fundraisers] is humorous.

Gibson: Oh, God, that's just a cattle call. And [you get a bill] unless you affirmatively take your name off the [proposed sponsor] list. You have to take your name off.

AMK: Do lawmakers really know who their contributors are?

Gibson: I think you generally know who they are, you are generally aware of who helped you. Some members will say they don't, but most members are generally aware.

AMK: Everyone says they absolutely hated raising money.

Gibson: That's true. It goes against everything you were raised to believe in. It would be one thing if you only had to do it every two years, but to raise the kind of dollars [required today], it's relentless. Everybody hates it.

AMK: Do they really all hate it as much as they say?

Gibson: Some people are so good at it you begin to think they must enjoy it. The question you really need to ask members is not whether they remember you gave to them, but whether they can remember who gave to their opponents. They can all recite that; they know that list, by heart. That one, they carry to the grave.

AMK: There have been all kinds of ideas, such as requiring the media to donate time.

Gibson: I just don't see that that's going to work. Let's say you gave them 30 minutes at 2 p.m. on a Saturday afternoon; that's not going to turn an election.

AMK: Well, what about limits on campaign contributions?

Gibson: That could require an amendment to the [Texas] constitution. It's just a real tough issue. After wrestling with it for 20 years, I've kind of come down on the side of making sure you report it all, requiring that it be very timely, and that you in fact use it for a campaign.

AMK: When you say, 'just disclose it all,' shouldn't it also tell you who the contributors are?

Gibson: That's not an issue for us, because people know who we are — but I do think that very rapid disclosure can be accomplished today.

AMK: Officeholder accounts. How long should someone keep one active?

Gibson: I hadn't really thought about that. I thought you had six years to dispose of it. I guess as long as you've got assets. I wonder what's happened to Bullock's money. [Editor's note: Bullock gave it all away, mostly to Baylor University, before he died.]

★   ★   ★

Transcript of interview with Gene Green, former Democratic Texas House and Texas Senate member, and now Congress member from Houston.

Anne Marie Kilday: These statistics on campaign finance in Texas make people question whether these numbers are healthy for democracy in Texas. What's your view of that?

Green: Well, when I was in the Legislature, I never had many people give me more than the federal limits, anyway. Although, I knew that was available, whether it's trial lawyers or that fellow in San Antonio [Dr. James Leininger] or some of the big Republican donors in Dallas, Houston and San Antonio, who will write the $20,000 or $25,000 checks. Far be it from me to say the federal system is far better than what we have in Texas, because I don't always feel that way. Yet, it does make you have a broader base, if you limit it to $1,000 and $5,000 per PAC. Of course, on the federal level, I have to raise astronomically more money than I did as a state senator, although as a state senator, I didn't have a really competitive election, except in '90, when I had a Republican who did fairly well. At the federal level, we have to raise anywhere from $350,000 to $400,000, and that's in pretty non-competitive districts. Now Ken Bentsen [also a Houston Democratic congressman] has to raise $1 million to $1.2 million, because that's a 50-50 district. It makes you broader; it makes you go to more people to get those $500 or $1,000 contributions.

AMK: But, on the federal level, do the limits force you to spend an inordinate amount of time raising money?

Green: Yeah, I spend a lot of time. I spend as much as other members do, but I've tried to limit myself to three fundraisers a year. When I was in the Legislature I had one in Austin and one in Houston, and now I have two in D.C. and one in Houston. Now, if I'm not raising money for myself, I'm raising it for the Democratic Congressional Campaign Committee. And, because we've been in the minority for a while, that takes up a lot of time, and we'll never be able to raise what the Republicans can raise.

Former Senator Gene Green:

"Their [big contributors'] influence probably depends on the officeholder, but it does bother me that you can say, 'I'm running for statewide office and will you write me a check for $100,000?' It does bother me."

AMK: Why?

Green: Typically, as Democrats, we don't have the higher-income resources. People say, 'You have labor and trial lawyers.' That's not as good as what Bill Archer [a now-retired Houston Republican congressman] can do in his district, where there are maybe 500 people who can write a $1,000 check and not bat an eye. In my district I've got some strong support, especially in the Hispanic business community, but nowhere near what you have in those high-income districts.

AMK: In addition to limits, the discussion turns to officeholder accounts in Texas. Is it good for people to have money stashed away?

Green: Well, that's considered a war chest, which they could hold on to for another campaign, [or] to run for something else. On the federal level most members give scholarships or give it to other members in $1,000 increments. I don't know whether officeholder accounts have restrictions. I think I had $30,000 in my state campaign account when I ran for Congress, and it was gone very quickly.

AMK: Does it concern you that statewide, roughly, 700 people and PACs have that much influence because they give almost half the money in Texas races?

Green: Their influence probably depends on the officeholder, but it does bother me that you can say, 'I'm running for statewide office and will you write me a check for $100,000?' It does bother me.

AMK: Does it buy access?

Green: I think it buys access and return calls. Hopefully, it doesn't — legally, it shouldn't — buy any votes. If somebody asks me and says, 'I supported you,' I immediately draw that line and say, 'I appreciated your support,' but I'll also listen to some-one who gave to my opponent. If you're in this as an elected official, I don't think it makes sense not to listen to someone who gave to your opponent.

AMK: The Legislature is so fiercely competitive. SD 3 in East Texas is an example, where they are going to spend between $3 and $4 million.

Green: Yes, it will be the most expensive Senate race in the country. There's anoth-er one in Pennsylvania, I understand, where there is a similar race. I sent $1,000 to [Democratic candidate David] Fisher. I'd really like to have that Senate balance go 16-15 Democratic next session. [The Texas Senate had a 16-15 Republican majority before the elections and remained that way after the 2000 election.]

AMK: Because of redistricting?

Green: Oh, yes.

AMK: Is this the first time we are seeing the national committees coming into Texas?

Green: I think we've had it a little in the past, but this is unprecedented. That's due to redistricting, and to the increased [party] competition. We raised a lot of money in Texas for the Democratic National Committee, both for congressional and legislative races. The goal is to leverage that money to help over in East Texas, where Max Sandlin and Ralph Hall [also Democratic congressmen] have opponents. We hope to get out a big Democratic vote.

AMK: When the dollars get this high, does it follow that it increases voter apathy?

Green: I don't know how to explain the decrease in voter participation across the country. With these exponential increases in spending, you'd think that if you are spending more money you'd have more commercials, you'd have more mail, you'd have more contact with people, and that would motivate them to vote. I think the negative campaigning is turning people off.

AMK: What is driving up the cost of campaigning?

Green: Obviously the cost of media has gone up dramatically. If I ever wanted to buy an ad in the Houston Chronicle it isn't cost-effective. I haven't priced it in years. We do so much polling now, and consultants. I never even had a consultant until I ran for Congress, and then in '92 I tried to hire all of them to keep them away from [Democratic primary opponent] Bennie [Reyes]. I hired Jack Martin, Dave Gold and Mark McKinnon out of Austin, and Dan McClung in Houston, but Bennie hired Emory and Young [also of Austin]. We're in a very competitive business and you want quality people. I just didn't have the $50,000 or I would've hired them, too.

AMK: When you first ran for the Legislature, how much did you spend?
Green: Oh, yeah, sure I remember. I had a primary and it was a knock-down drag-out, with a run-off and then the general election with an opponent. It cost me $5,500, and that was only one mail-out. We actually hand-addressed our mail-out, of about 15,000. Talk about a labor of love by a lot of people. That was long before computers. When I ran for state Senate in 1985, I spent about $125,000. That was cheap. I remember people telling me I got off cheap [to beat fellow House member Tony Polumbo].

AMK: What about now when you run for Congress?
Green: I did not have a primary opponent, but I do have a Republican opponent, and I am contracted to spend about $200,000.

AMK: That's not much for a Congress seat.
Green: No, it's not, but we are doing a lot more to build up and redo all the lists I have. We are doing a real grass-roots effort with mailings only. At least one in Spanish. That doesn't include any media. If I do any media, I will do a Spanish-language station that in Houston costs less, but reaches as many viewers almost as Channel 13, the top-rated station.

AMK: During your days in the Legislature, did you witness a vote influenced by a campaign contribution?
Green: I don't know that I can make that judgment call. I will say that if they were my opponents on an issue, I think they were too swayed by their campaign contributors. In all seriousness, I think, by and large, while I served there you didn't see that, maybe with rare exceptions, and those people are no longer there. But nobody ever

told me, 'I'm doing this because somebody gave me $1,000 or $5,000.'

AMK: What, if anything, would you change?

Green: One good thing Texas does is there is no fundraising 30 days before and during the session. I think that's a good thing. It makes you do your job without worrying about money. I would put some limits on it. There are some of my Republican colleagues here who want the federal limits raised to $2,000. I don't know what's ideal, but I think you should have some type of limits on the amount an individual can contribute to your campaign. And, of course, our fight in Congress is always: Once we come up with a campaign-finance reform, they always find a way to get around it. Such as, soft money. I've taken soft money, because this is a competitive business. Limits ought to be real limits. And then we do run into concerns about free speech. Yet you really ought to be able to trace those PAC contributions to groups like Texans for Good Government, which tells you nothing. You ought to know, if John Doe gave them money, who John Doe is, and it ought to be on the Internet. The technology that has helped on campaigns should help track campaign finance. I just don't want to scare off somebody from running for the Legislature.

★　★　★

Transcript of interview with John Hirschi, former Democratic House member from Wichita Falls, and businessman.

Anne Marie Kilday: You support changing the Texas campaign finance system. Why?

Hirschi: The Texas system is just so wide open. The federal situation is terrible, and the Texas system makes the federal system look like the Golden Rule.

AMK: In what way? Because there are no limits?

Hirschi: Yeah, it's wide open. There are no limits; there's a little period of time when you have to hold off [raising money], but other than that you can take whatever you want. It obviously means the lobby has even more power in Texas than it does on the federal level, since there is no control at all. Obviously, in the court system it's particularly bad, [because] people are taking money while they are trying cases and could be making rulings on them. I've always been a very staunch supporter of very strict campaign contribution limits. I think we should have better filing of campaign contributions, so people can't do this stuff where all that money hits in the last few days of a campaign and nobody knows where all that dirty money is from, and who it's from.

AMK: What else needs to be done?

Hirschi: Obviously, because of the constitution, we run into some problems there with [limits]. I'm all for public financing of campaigns. I think that's the only answer to getting control of spending and giving non-incumbents a chance of being elected to office. I think one of the other problems is [concrete information on candidates' stands on issues], and Project Vote Smart, which has been working at the federal level for some time, is getting into that. Although I'm not sure that [information] is widely disseminated in the press. My own congressman and the [U.S.] senators…I don't know whether that stuff gets in the press in the big cities, but in the smaller cities, like Wichita Falls, it's not. To do a story before an election telling how all the organizations rate your representatives would seem like a no-brainer, to avail themselves [the media] and the public of that information.

Former Rep. John Hirschi:

"The Texas system is just so wide open. The federal situation is terrible, and the Texas system makes the federal system look like the Golden Rule."

AMK: So, the press itself could do a better job monitoring and reporting campaign contributions?

Hirschi: Yes. I don't think there's any doubt. I follow the Dallas paper; I don't read it as extensively as I did when I was in office, but that hasn't jumped out at me in the headlines. It's so easy; their work has already been done for them. It's just a matter of reporting what liberal to arch-conservative organizations and special issue organizations rate legislators. I think the public could be much better informed if they knew Joe Blow had a zero environment record and a 100 percent record with the chemical companies. People may choose to vote for the chemical companies, but at least they would have some idea of how their representatives have been voting.

AMK: Do you think the law is strong enough in Texas on reporting requirements at the Ethics Commission?

Hirschi: Yeah, where are they with electronic reporting? It is the law.

AMK: As I understand it, it's now on-line. I don't know if there have been glitches.

Hirschi: Well, one of the problems that we had in the past was we had to go over to the commission. Now I'm out of date, but the last time we tried to get some financial information we had to send somebody out there with a roll of quarters, and sit there and plug the money in for each page. That was just absurd — the cost and amount of time it took to get that information. I don't know whether that information is now available electronically. [Editor's note: Most of it is, under a 1999 statute.] My first race in 1990 cost about $50,000, and my opponent spent about $100,000.

AMK: So money is not always the determining factor?

Hirschi: Absolutely not, but it was pretty close.

AMK: Did your campaign operation include volunteers, or has campaigning just become a political industry?

Hirschi: Well, it's some of both. It depends on the district and the amount of money a person has in their war chest. Back when I ran the first time, it was a much lower budget and we had a volunteer phone bank; and now it seems like nobody, that I am aware of, does volunteer phone banks. And, a lot of door-to-door knocking—that was a major factor in my race. There are still those who believe in that door-to-door approach, in a fairly compact district.

AMK: How hard was it for you to ask for money?

Hirschi: I've never been very good at that. Fortunately, I didn't have an opponent after my first race. It's something that is abhorrent to me. I did finance part of my original race and did fundraisers over the next three terms, like, say, one a term. I finally retired that debt to myself over the next six years. There should be some limits on personal financing of campaigns. It's becoming more and more popular, with lots of guys running for statewide races putting millions and millions of their own money into their campaigns, just buying the race.

AMK: Is that what it amounts to? Buying the race?

Hirschi: Well, sure. If I've got unlimited pockets and can spend unlimited amounts on television, mail-outs, and whatever else, it is extremely difficult for anybody to stay competitive. What we're seeing is these races, every cycle, get a lot more expensive. It just seems like there is no limit on the spending. It seems like our representatives in Congress are really spending all their time raising money, rather than spending their time really dealing with the issues.

AMK: Does it follow that big money translates into voter apathy?

Hirschi: I can't prove that. I think people hear constantly in the press that these elections are being bought by major special interests. And I think some of the data coming out of the polling today are showing large numbers of people saying [an election] won't impact their lives. So, if they have that attitude, why would they bother to vote? People are apathetic because they know that large special interests are controlling the agenda of both political parties.

AMK: So, what's the answer?

Hirschi: Public financing of campaigns. Come up with some kind of formula. I don't think it's going to happen in the foreseeable future, but it's the only way you can allow a person of modest means that may have extremely good credentials to get into the race. Another thing, which I don't think has ever been corrected, is not requiring a person to divulge the actual amount in a campaign account, that carry-over from prior campaigns. I think that's just terrible. If I'm sitting there with half a million dollars from prior races and I go out and start having these fundraisers to add to a lot more money, it's not fair to contributors, number one. And, it is certainly a very newsworthy item.

AMK: Individual limits? Would you favor that or oppose that?

Hirschi: I am very much in favor of that. I cannot imagine why a state race could not easily be restricted to no more than federal law. A very modest place to start would be the limit on federal campaign contributions. Those things are pretty strict. Or if it's $500 per cycle, that limits it to $1,000 [for a primary and a general election], which is not a small amount of change. But, in Texas, where a person can give $5,000 or $25,000 or whatever to a guy, it's just totally crazy.

AMK: Did you ever see money make the difference in a decision or a vote?

Hirschi: Well, I can't point to any specific person. Obviously, legislators are driven by lots of factors. If I've got a dirty [utility or manufacturing] plant in my district that employs a bunch of people, I'm probably going to do everything I can to see that no legislation is passed to hurt that industry. At the same time, I think you could look at contributions to the legislator from that district and see that he has received contributions from that industry. But, you know, whether it's a 100 percent surety to say it's to save the jobs or the money, it's probably a combination of both. As a for instance, in my last session we were trying to get the grandfathered pollution plants of utilities to come up to compliance with the standards adopted in 1973. And those legislators who had...oh, who was it that passed away so suddenly?...[the late Rep. Dan Kubiak, a Democrat from Rockdale] had the dirtiest plant in the state — Alcoa — in his district. He let me know that he was going to fight tooth-and-nail to keep out a tax on pollution. That's tax reform...I had an amendment that would have added taxing pollution, which would have given polluters an incentive to clean up. And everybody who had a dirty coal plant, or Alcoa — I never seriously thought it would clean up — I'm sure they would say it was jobs. But, they had those political contributions. I guess I can't say the money made a difference. I will give you another for instance: I've carried tobacco bills. I do know when we were in committee hearings on one bill, the tobacco lobbyist was a friend of the committee chairman. Well, I just happened to look up and see eye contact between the committee chairman and the lobbyist, who was shaking his head, and that was the end of that bill. It was pretty obvious where the power was — it wasn't in the Legislature, it was in the lobby.

★   ★   ★

Transcript of interview with Mike Martin, former Democratic House member from Galveston, who later lost a race for the Texas Senate and who now practices law.

Anne Marie Kilday: Sam Kinch and I are working on this book about campaign finance…

Martin: I've heard about this book, from Fred Lewis [the president of the publisher, Campaigns for People]. [With him] we are suing over Texas' system of judicial selection, claiming the judicial system is unconstitutional because of contributions made in judicial races.

AMK: So, is campaign contributing unconstitutional in the Legislature as well?

Martin: The Legislature has got its own share of problems. I don't think it's unconstitutional on the legislative end, but I do think there is desperate need for reform.

AMK: And what are those reforms?

Martin: There is the fact that the cost of legislative elections is out of control. As a consequence of that, the dynamics of serving in the Legislature and running for office have placed too much importance on money and fund-raising, which could be true for Congress as well. So the solution—this is a pretty big question—the issue needs to be how to curtail the influence of money, either by public finance or campaign finance limits, or guaranteed access to publicly licensed venues, such as radio and TV. Things of that nature that will remove the element of cost. When I ran for the Senate I spent over $800,000. My opponent spent over $1 million. And, for a state Senate seat that's absurd. That's ridiculous — and he [then-Republican Sen. Jerry Patterson, R-Pasadena, now a lobbyist] and I both agree on that. My Senate race is a classic example of a race that is totally out of control. I had contributions…I don't think I got anything as large as he, but as I recall Jerry got a contribution of $100,000, which is just ridiculous. That creates such a strong appearance of impropriety to the general public, when they see that kind of political contribution. All you have to do is report it. Don Henley [rock musician] gave me $25,000; the Texas Trial Lawyers gave me $75,000. So, the same could be said for me. That is $100 grand on my end. Texans for Lawsuit Reform gave Jerry $100 grand. Any way you look at it, that kind of contribution…at that level…even if a legislator/member can say that doesn't affect my vote, even if he can say that with a straight face, it creates an appearance to the public that votes can be bought. And, that is undermining the public's faith in the political process, both on the legislative end and the congressional end. The only thing you have to do under the law right now is just report it. So what the hell? Big deal — you report it.

AMK: And is there the potential for inaccuracy?

Martin: I think there is that potential for inaccuracy, because the Texas Ethics Commission isn't the greatest on policing this; and, it wasn't until this year when electronic filing first went into effect, the public didn't even have access to this, which was a good reform. Hell, the public didn't even have access to this information unless a newspaper reported it. They wouldn't know unless a newspaper picked up on it and reported it, and the only newspapers that did that…well, I can't think of any. I don't recall reading a newspaper report, at least not very frequently, on who gave what to whom.

AMK: And when you read the reports, you may know what TREPAC or IBAT is?

Martin: Right, the general public doesn't have a clue [about the names of PACs].

AMK: You need a decoder ring?

Martin: Absolutely. That's a real problem, but it's more than identifying the parties. You identify the parties, you identify LIST, which is the TTLA [trial lawyers] PAC that gave Mike Martin $50 grand. Let's say the public figures it out—well, it's still too damn much money. A $50,000 contribution from a PAC, or Dick Weekley or Texans for Lawsuit Reform, whatever their PAC is called, turns around and gives Jerry Patterson $100,000; it's too much money. It's too damn much money. No person who has any sense about what's right and wrong in this world will believe that kind of money doesn't influence a vote. And, it does. If it does nothing else, it creates the appearance. That appearance alone is cause for concern; because, it is the public's trust in the government that is at stake here, and the public has lost its trust in the government. In big ways, the apathy is all over the place.

AMK: Do you think the apathy follows from the cynicism of big money?

Martin: Yes, absolutely no doubt in my mind. There are all kinds of indications of voter apathy — looking first at voter turnout in the election cycles of the 1990s.

AMK: Tell me why big money makes them apathetic.

Martin: Big money makes them apathetic, because they don't feel that their vote makes any difference. They don't feel they have any control over an issue. It's not really a matter of who you vote for and the impact of that vote, it's a matter of who raised the most money to buy the most commercials, to say the most bad, mean things about the other guy. That's what it's about. People know that. So, they see these big contributions, and they see how it's spent on campaigns and they don't have any ability…they don't have the time to figure out the specific distinctions of the influence of that money — it's just going all over the place. So, of course, somebody is going to get apathetic about that kind of a system in a big way. Anybody who says otherwise, who says, 'Oh, the voters aren't that apathetic' or 'Oh, it's not that much' or 'Oh, it doesn't mean that much influence from money,' is just lying through their teeth. And, they know better.

When I was in office, the lobby's biggest complaint after the Ethics Reform session of 1991—in the ethics reform session of '91 we did away with the lunches and the golf trips and the hunting trips, and that was good reform. But, what a lobbyist would tell you was, 'Well, it placed much more emphasis on writing the check, as opposed to creating a relationship through some ski trip' and they don't like that. It placed much greater emphasis on the need for the check and the need for the money for these campaign coffers than anything else did. It just created more emphasis on money.

AMK: That's interesting. Instead of buying your lunch…

Martin: Well, it was more than buying lunch — it was the parties, the trips, developing this 'good old boy,' you know, 'buddy system,' with all these perks. Which was, for a lobbyist, probably a lot more fun for him and a lot cheaper than having to just walk in and give a $5,000 check to a member of the Legislature. As a consequence of the elimination of all that stuff, from a legislator's standpoint, they looked to the money as being far more important from lobbyists because that's really all they are good for. [He laughed.]

AMK: That's kind of harsh.

Martin: Well, it's true. Now, I can't say all lobbyists are bad. I had lots of lobbyists in my office when I was in the House. Some are very knowledgeable and some are trustworthy. And, it's those who are trustworthy and who are good at communicating their position, as well as being fair in their communication about an issue, that make them worthwhile. And that was the second thing that was said to me when I was in office: There was more emphasis placed on the [campaign] check and there was more emphasis placed on the hard issues that were being debated in a particular bill. Which they didn't have to work so hard on when they were out gallivanting around, buddy-buddying with different people. They didn't have to work so hard and say, 'Okay, here are the issues.' Instead you had your friend [and] you'd been on a bunch of trips with him, [and] he said, 'Look, this is important to me.' Based on that friendship, a legislator would just kind of vote one way or the other. And now, because that's missing, the issue does become more important. So, ethics reform was good for that, but it did place more emphasis on the [campaign] check.

I mention that lobbyist [angle], not only from the standpoint of being a legislator before and after ethics reform, but I was on the staff for a variety of members of the Legislature. Back in the days when the 'good old boy', 'buddy system' in the Legislature was in its hot days. Back in the late '70's and early '80's, when Texas was rich and the Legislature was nothing but a party from the time it went into session until the time it adjourned, and the special session was foreign to anybody. Nobody had to worry about anything. It was nothing but fun. So we have made some steps forward, but as a consequence of making those steps forward, eliminating that…we put more emphasis on the check.

AMK: So you have to be careful when you take on campaign finance reform as well?

Martin: Right. What you have to be able to accomplish in campaign finance reform is that this is a constitutional issue, as well as a practical issue. You have to accomplish campaign finance reform without shutting down the ability of an officeholder or a candidate to get his message out. Because the argument against it is, if you shut down or limit financing of races you are basically violating First Amendment rights.

You are violating and eliminating the ability of a candidate to convey his message to the people. He has that right, and it is important. I agree with all of that, but it seems to me, and this may be a naïve observation in terms of political feasibility, it seems to me there may be ways to fix that. You know, we license our public airwaves, both on radio and TV. Companies make a lot of money on that right to broadcast and that is a right, and they have a public service [standard] to meet that right. So access to those airwaves, basically by [the federal government] saying, 'Okay, we are going to allot so much [air time] to this office and so much to this office for candidates to get their message out' — I mean, it could be more involved than that [to implement]. You know it doesn't cost anybody any money, except maybe a TV station. So what? Big deal. And, it still allows a candidate to get his message out without having to go out and raise the kind of money it takes to buy a commercial in the Houston market, for example.

AMK: What makes you think viewers would stay tuned in?
Martin: Well, you'd have to control that proposal with some controls that would guarantee [air] space at certain times. You know, you can't guarantee all that space at four o'clock in the morning. You'd have to control that issue, however it is dealt with, by guaranteeing some access during the news, some access during prime time, and some time during the afternoon. Those are details. It would take a lot of effort to put together a campaign finance reform proposal that would work, and, number two, that you could get a consensus on. I would be surprised that either could happen at this point, as there's just not enough drive to do it.

AMK: You don't think so?
Martin: I don't think we're there yet. I mean, not in the Legislature. I think we're closer in Congress than in the Legislature, and we're a long way away from it in Congress. The attractiveness of John McCain [as a presidential candidate], I think, is a good example. I think the reason he got votes was because at least he stood for some kind of campaign reform, not very good campaign reform, but at least for something. I think that was a signal from the voters.

AMK: It takes a while for ideas to catch on.

Martin: Yep. [In the 2000 presidential election]…I think there will be a high degree of apathy. I think part of the problem will be the cost of the races, and the other part is soft money and the almost corruptive aspect of soft money. I had a candidate, whom I will leave unnamed, call me last week and say, 'I have to raise X amount of soft money for this effort and that effort. And that's just above and beyond my own candidacy. We've just got to have that soft money.' It just requires candidates to go out and ask anybody they can find for money — anybody who can write a check. How easy is it to start looking at the fine line of black and white, and distinguishing the really hard truths about issues, when everybody under the sun who is related to that issue has given you a hefty campaign contribution? It's got to have some impact on it.

AMK: When you were in the Legislature, honestly, did money influence a vote?
Martin: No, it didn't. One of my votes, it didn't. Did money influence a vote? Yes. I can't give you a specific example of a legislator. But, when I look systemically at voting patterns, and I look at the kinds of lobby groups that needed those votes and compare them to lobby groups that were giving money, it was the lobby groups giving money that won, against the lobby groups that didn't give any money at all. I think if you did an analysis you'd prove that almost as a matter of certainty. And, quite frankly, when you look at it from an issue standpoint.… I was an environmentalist, an environmental legislator. But environmental groups don't give money [to legislators]. The green-oriented people. There aren't any environmental groups out there giving money. On the other hand, there's the Texas Chemical Council; there's the oil and gas interests; there's the electrical utility industry; there's the hazardous waste interests — that's four right there. The amount of money they have pumped into the Legislature is phenomenal. And when those issues come up, straight up, those guys, the big guys, win all the time. It's only when they're not paying attention that an environmental piece of legislation might accidentally pass. And it did in 1991, only because the climate was right and nobody was really paying attention. So, if you were to do an analysis, you'd prove my point that money does influence votes, because the votes that are winning are the lobbies and the lobby organizations that are pumping lots of dollars into the Legislature. Does it buy votes on an individual basis? There isn't a legislator around who's going to admit that to you.

But you can look at it from another standpoint: Maybe it's not buying a vote, but it's buying a philosophy of a legislator at the time he is running. A group contributes to a legislator that they know is philosophically aligned with them, so that legislator is going to go and vote in their way because they share common philosophies. An example? Me. I'm a trial lawyer. I represent plaintiffs. When the trial bar gives me money, it's with some degree of confidence that generally I am going to be an advocate for their position. Now, the funny thing about that is, when you get there and you end up not doing that, then people pay attention. *Texas Monthly* put me on the Ten Best list in my first session. I think that was one of the reasons they did that, because I ended up taking some trial lawyer money. Then I ended up taking some trial lawyer stuff [legislation] and basically ripping it to pieces. So, there is always balance and there is always conscience...personal ethics. I think a lot of people in that building have those standards, but it still doesn't deny the fact that there is an influence of money.

Former Rep. Mike Martin:

"There was a vote up in committee related to shrimping and it was a close vote, and my boss [when I was a legislative aide] leaned over to me and said, 'Who's given me more money?'"

Now, when I worked in the Legislature, I'll never forget. This was 20 years ago. I'll never forget sitting in a committee meeting. I was clerk to the Natural Resources Committee and, uh, this was after [the defeat of Democratic Sen.] Babe [Schwartz]. I was working for [former El Paso Democratic Sen.] Tati Santiesteban. He was chair of the committee. There was a vote up in committee related to shrimping and it was a close vote, and my boss leaned over to me and said, 'Who's given me more money?' When he asked me, I said, 'Beats the hell out of me.' I was shocked. Of course, I was young, 21 years old. I was a pup. Still, I was shocked because I had worked for Babe before then. That is one specific example, and I have a very clear recollection of that. I started off in the Legislature working for Babe Schwartz, and there was nobody who was straighter. There was no greater mentor for me, illustrating to me what it was like to be in the Legislature and stand on the issues and advocate your position on the issues. He was the only guy I ever knew, then or since that time, who prohibited lobbyists from coming into his office. That was a rule. A staff rule: No lobbyists were allowed in the office. And, as a young freshman at UT, it was always interesting to me how there was never anybody in Babe's office. I'd go into other senators' offices and they'd always be crowded with people sitting around and I always wondered what they were doing. And, I'd walk in Babe's office and it was always very businesslike. The only people sitting outside were people who came up from the district. It was amazing to me to work then for Santiesteban after that, who was the antithesis of that, who almost pandered to the lobby. Back in those days, it was clear to me that money influenced the system. It was amazing to me that Babe was able to win, even if by narrow margins. If I'd chosen to stay where I was [in the House], I'd still be there. I had 68 percent margins of victory. The money-raising component when I was in the House was a factor, but because I was in a safe House seat I wasn't totally focused on raising money. Until I ran for the Senate, and I learned how horrible it was. I mean, the TV buy I made in the Senate [campaign], I spent $200,000 for that one single investment. That's obscene.

★　★　★

Transcript of interview with Parker McCollough, former Democratic House member from Georgetown, and now an Austin lobbyist for Entergy, a power company.

Anne Marie Kilday: Let's talk about campaign finance reform.

McCollough: There's never been a great hue and cry for campaign finance reform here, has there? Well, right when we created the Ethics Commission in '91, there was the impression that the sun was going to shine on the process. And, it has been too slow, but has there ever been a clamor at the Legislature to get them moving faster?

AMK: I'm not sure there has been at the Legislature, because people don't know what they don't know. If you go to the Ethics Commission, you can look at the list of PACs, you might understand that Texas Good Roads is the highway contractor lobby, but there are these funny names. You look at the contributor list and it's not all that revealing. You'd hope to find an occupation, right?

McCollough: Yes. For the filings that I make at the Ethics Commission for our PAC, I file a monthly report showing the amount, the name and maybe the address. It's generally payroll deductions of company employees who gave to the PAC. If you go to the realtor PAC, which I ran for four years, you'll see 8 to 10,000 people who gave to the PAC, and the filing is just a computer print-out.

AMK: That's not always all that telling.

McCollough: I appreciate that.

AMK: In the last election, there was $121 million spent statewide, which includes all statewide candidates on down to the Legislature, and one-half of that $121 million came from fewer than 700 sources.

McCollough: Is that individuals, not PACs? Who are they? How did I miss 'em?

AMK: It's both, but is that good for democracy?

McCollough: You didn't call to argue with me. I would ask the question, 'Is that bad?'

You can paint a pretty bad picture of it, but are those people buying elections? I mean, 'Is the process being tainted,' is the question. And, I don't know; I'd have to really think about that. I was involved in the '94 election, before the tort reform session, and Dick Weekley [who organized the first high-dollar PAC behind tort reform] was so heavily involved in that. I guess a question would be, 'Did his participation make a difference? Did his participation and the dollars he paid out make a difference on that issue?' I think you'd have to say, 'Yeah, it made a difference.' They were able to win a Senate race in East Texas — that's when [Republican] Michael Galloway beat [long-time Democratic Sen.] Carl Parker. So maybe it did. And, the question is, 'Is that bad?' My initial reaction is, as long as you've got a Legislature of elected officials who have to stand on the ballot every two years or four years, maybe it's not bad.

AMK: And what about the fact that 80 percent of the average legislator's contributions are from outside his own district?
McCollough: What do I think about that? Well, I beat up on a guy when I was elected for taking money from all these out-of-district folks. The next thing I know, I've got money coming in and I'm raising money from all the same people. It's not a pure process.... You know, when you do your reports, you want to list every individual person who bought a $25 ticket to your barbecue to help cover up some of that stuff. To give it a little balance, and the perception of balance.

AMK: Is all this because the nature of races has changed? It's not a door-to-door deal?
McCollough: It costs money, but hasn't it always? If the thrust of the argument is that we can run honest elections without money, I don't know. You run into constitutional issues. Are you telling me I can't give [now-retired Sen.] Drew Nixon $2,000, because I've got the money and you don't? I've not researched this at all. I think any campaign-finance issues run into the threshold question of the constitutional issues.

AMK: Yes, but there is the federal limit. And, we do have the Texas judicial limits. Now you could say that drives members of Congress to spending an inordinate amount of time raising money...
McCollough: All the time. All the time. Where I get a little concerned, and where I think there is a real perception problem is that money is being raised while issues

are being debated and voted on. The one great provision of our [Texas] campaign finance system is there can be no campaign fundraising starting 30 days [from] and then through the legislative session. That was done before I got here, but there was that special session where [East Texas poultry magnate] Bo Pilgrim was out there giving money on the Senate floor. My impression was the press did a pretty good job addressing that issue, so they are not handing money out in the Capitol any more.

AMK: When you were running, how hard was it to ask for money?

McCollough: Everybody will tell you that it is the worst part of the job. And, I'm not talking about having the coffees or get-togethers, and those fundraisers back in the district, but I was trained early, early in the process to get on the telephone and work the [lobby] book. I hated it. I'd rather have a root canal than sit down with someone with a phone list, and they'd be sitting on the other side of the desk—'This is Joe Bill. He gave $500 in March of this year and he gave $1,000 to so-and-so, so you need to ask him for at least $1,000.' It's horrible. It is just…members will tell you they hate it.

AMK: Members also say they don't know who gave money to them. Is that true?

McCollough: Some of them, I might believe that. Some, who are capable of raising a bucket of money — committee chairmen, say — may not have known the contributors. There were times when I didn't have a clue where these people came from. You put yourself on the ballot, you get yourself elected, and these are people who have some interest in the Legislature when they make a contribution. The fact that they don't make some tie, some way to make the connection when they get it to you, is their fault. Maybe you just get a contribution from some PAC without a lobbyist's name on it or the name of a government affairs person that you know…yeah, you don't always know where it came from.

AMK: Don't you send thank-you notes?

McCollough: Absolutely. You have to be very disciplined. [As a contributor] I don't expect it, but I always appreciate it. It shows me that person is disciplined and doing the right thing. While I'm cynical enough, it never influenced me; a lot of people it does. A lot of people who get a thank-you note from their state rep. or senator, it means something.

AMK: How has the role of money increased in campaigns? Your first race?

McCollough: My first race, 12 years ago, cost $165,000 for a primary, a run-off and the general election. They are more sophisticated now. I had a consultant and I had a campaign manager. A lot of these folks don't have campaign managers, but I think you are starting to see more and more sophistication in the training programs the parties put on — how to raise money, how to get your message out, what that message is...how [to recognize] what your opponent did or didn't do, how to mobilize volunteers...things of that nature. In the first go-round, I had a very sophisticated and dedicated bunch of volunteers who would work at the phone bank, and people like that. They've invested their time or money, so they feel like they've got a little ownership — and they do. I mean, you never forget those people who stood up with you, at a time when it may not have been the smart thing to do, and backed you. It creates a bond and an ability to work with them. By the time I left the House I had graduated to paid phone-bankers and I didn't like that, but it was the nature of that particular campaign, and it was easier to do it. I did not have to worry about getting people to the phone bank. For $1,500 to this firm, we got a week of phone-banking between the hours of five and nine p.m. You are seeing a lot of that as it's a whole lot easier to do and manage. People are just busy.

Former Rep. Parker McCullough:

"But, sure, money has always had an influence on the public's view of politicians. So, yeah, I do think there is a pretty good deal of cynicism that translates over into voter apathy — all the way down the ballot."

AMK: The idea of campaign finance limits...is there any way it would pass in Texas?

PM: Sam Kinch coined the phrase that, 'The Legislature is like Pearl Harbor — nobody starts moving 'til the bombs start falling.' In '91, you had all the stories about the trips, the cozy relationships, and the need to have a bill to address that. You had a series of stories in '89, '90 and '91, you had a speaker [Gib Lewis] who was letting that stuff happen and who was subsequently under indictment. Everybody was reading about these things that the lobby was doing. It created the perception that there was undue influence — that there was unfair influence, I should say. We had a big outcry, and it was an outcry. It was driven by newspaper editorial boards, it was driven by Smitty [Public Citizen of Texas lobbyist Tom Smith] — the [urge] that the process needed changing. Do we have that now? I don't know that we do.

AMK: Do people seem more blase about politics?

McCollough: Well, sure. Look at how many people voted in the last election. It's very, very upsetting to have seen the drop-off of people voting in the election. They're talking about the national [party] conventions coming up and how few people will be watching [and even after network news coverage was scaled down]. When I was a kid, I remember the '60's. Maybe that's because I was a political junkie even then…. It was pretty high drama — the '68 Democratic convention. I remember I was a junior or senior in high school, and I remember those Chicago cops beat the living crap out of those kids, who were maybe no more than two years older than I was. It really takes your breath away to think about…. I don't know if we're doing a very good job of educating and involving our children in the electoral process as our parents did. It's probably got something to do with the economy, and we don't have a Cold War any more. We're not under a threat. It was a different time. The interest in politics has really changed. Or they just say, 'Oh, they're all a bunch of crooks.'

AMK: Is money part of a reason for that cynicism?

McCollough: Uh-huh, sure. And, the parties have gotten so partisan. I think one reason [Gov. George W.] Bush has appeal is that he's gotten a good message out that he works pretty well with both sides. I don't know, it's going to be interesting to see how that plays out. In the early '90s, look how [President Bill] Clinton worked the money issue. It's going to be very interesting to see how people view Al Gore's involvement in fundraising. There could be people going to jail over fundraising. I think both sides…you had the Whitewater issue, and then the Republicans getting popped on the other side. But, sure, money has always had an influence on the public's view of politicians. So, yeah, I do think there is a pretty good deal of cynicism that translates over into voter apathy — all the way down the ballot.

*   *   *

Transcript of interview with Bob McFarland, former Republican House member and state Senator from Arlington, who is now a lawyer and a lobbyist.

Anne Marie Kilday: Let's start with the figures...$121 million spent statewide on elections in 1998.

McFarland: Funding has changed so significantly in the decade since I left office. I think I had one Austin fundraiser in my 15 years — and I didn't even put it on. Some other people said, 'You need to have a fundraiser [because] you have never asked for funds.' They held a fundraiser for me. American Airlines had mechanical trouble, and I got there after the thing. Since I've left office, I am amazed at the cost of campaigns; the money spent in campaigns; the size of contributions solicited and expected; and the amount of officeholder and campaign reserves that are being maintained. I noticed yesterday in the Dallas Morning News that [Sen.] Royce West has purchased 15 billboards in Dallas County to advertise his student grant program — [the one] the state has for students who have achieved certain grade-point averages and are eligible for grants to Texas colleges. They are going unused because there are not that many students who know about it. And, I want to tell you, 15 billboards...Royce paid for it out of his officeholder account. That's sure a hell of a lot better than what most of them used their officeholder accounts for, but the fact that you would even have an officeholder account of that consequence amazes me. And, they all have them.

It used to be a $1,000 sponsorship would give you platinum status at anybody's fundraiser, and five [thousand] would get you the same status at the governor's. Now you talk five digits, six digits to even get your name on the program. I know, from a lobby standpoint, as you talk to the lobby, somebody has got to get a handle on this. Of all my clients, only one has a PAC. I don't think there's a member anywhere, whether it's the Legislature or the Texas congressional delegation, that doesn't appreciate a $50 contribution from Ma and Pa Jones. Or, even if they don't have an opponent, they know their success is reflective of their campaign war chest.

AMK: Should there be limits?

McFarland: My recollection is that the courts have struck down as unconstitutional…[a limit on the] amount that a candidate can give to himself. What do you do? Do you put a limit on the amounts that a person can make [contribute] to a campaign?

AMK: What's your feeling about what's driving the size of contributions?

McFarland: No doubt you are probably going to see [in the year 2000] the most expensive legislative race in this country's history right here in Senate District 3 [deep East Texas, from Palestine to The Woodlands]. Generically, campaigns have become so expensive. More importantly, there is the supposition that that race may well [determine partisan] control of the Texas Senate, and the race and spending there is already at fever pitch. I'll bet you that there will be more spending in that race than was spent on a governor's race, [by] both sides, 10 years ago. Members tell me that the cost of campaigning has increased, media costs as well as consultant costs. I never had any consultants; back when I was running few people had consultants. Now, you hire your campaign consultants at the same time you file your campaign treasurer. The campaign consultants are not only very expensive, but they are trying to maintain a track record and they believe you've got to spend to assure that you are successful. There is also the theory that if you spend a lot of money now and win by a margin of 70 percent, you've saved yourself a lot of money down the line. So you're seeing people that have minimal opposition spending a lot of money. Then you have a situation where, 'oops, somebody slipped up on me.'

AMK: What about television?

McFarland: There's no doubt that television is used now in lesser races than it was before, and it's awfully expensive. But it's one of those things — 'If my opponent does it, then I've got to do it.'

AMK: Your first race [for the House], what did it cost?

McFarland: Something tells me $40,000. It was a very hotly contested race. That was 1975.

AMK: That's still pretty expensive. What about your last race [for re-election to the

Senate]?

McFarland: I didn't have an opponent. It would have probably been nominal — some mailings, I would guess, [a total of] $10,000 or $15,000. I can remember when $50,000 in a House race and $100,000 in a Senate race was a significant amount. Now it's four-fold that; you're seeing $500,000 in House races and millions in Senate races.

AMK: It was suggested to me that those ethics reforms of the early '90s — with the ski trips and lavish parties, doing away with all of that — put more emphasis on the [campaign] check.

McFarland: I hadn't thought of that. Obviously it cleared up that money for contributions. That suggestion may have some merit, if you're a PAC and your lobbyist can't take a member to the Super Bowl or the Byron Nelson [golf tournament], where you have a chance to meet and greet, you do it now by money, i.e., campaign contributions. That may well be the case with those PACs, the companies that used to utilize the junket, for want of a better term. The average, non-corporate type lobby…it may well be that they spend more on contributions because they don't do the travel and entertainment. I'm not sure that's the cause or the reason for the large contributions. I think it's the cost of campaigning, the cost of serving and the desire of most officeholders to have a large reserve in an officeholder account, because now a member flying to another member's fundraiser uses their own funds or uses their officeholder funds. And, too, to me what's unique is the size of the contributions that officeholders are making to other campaigns. They are accumulating funds not just because of the cost of office-holding and for campaigning, but for charitable contributions and campaign contributions to colleagues. It surprises me, when you look at a candidate's contributors and you suddenly see from Senator 'So and So,' a $10,000 contribution…[or] look at some of the contributions that the senators are making to [Gov. George W.] Bush's presidential race. You see them making contributions in their districts, underwriting the political women's clubs, and things like that.

AMK: Did anybody [in the Legislature] ever give to you [as a re-election candidate]?

McFarland: Well, it wasn't going on when I was there. I was there when you could junket; that was a hell of a lot more fun… It's true that my golf game went to hell if the ball didn't have a corporate logo on it, and hell, six months out of office I was having to buy my own golf balls. I always joked that when I took up the game if I couldn't afford the balls I wouldn't continue to play. I remember this one time we were out playing and Bob Davis [a Republican House member at the time] hit his ball in the water, and then he did it again. So Davis turns around to a lobbyist and says, 'Give me another ball,' and the lobbyist says, 'Bob, these balls are kind of expensive.' And Davis says, 'If you can't afford the balls, you shouldn't have taken up the game.'

AMK: Well, what if you [as an incumbent legislator] contributed to a person [running for the Legislature]? If somebody had given you money, would that be okay with them?

McFarland: Why do you make a campaign contribution? Hopefully, because the person you are contributing to is the better-qualified candidate for the office and you want to see him in that office. Or, you contribute because you want to see him win and you want to be sure that if he does win, then you've been a contributor. Most would probably say they don't care how a candidate spends that money to further his relationship within his constituency, or if he gave money to a colleague, whether it's for a speaker's race or a lieutenant governor's race. I don't think that a contributor, a knowledgeable contributor, probably cares. The problem is, it's become the accepted way, or modus operandi.

AMK: Do contributions buy access?

McFarland: Sure. Positively. Absolutely. Anybody who says it doesn't, doesn't understand politics.

AMK: And you know who gave you money?

McFarland: I'm probably a lot different from most officeholders. I wasn't a [former Atty. Gen.] Jim Mattox where, if you had an appointment, he had your [political information] card right next to him...in the file on his desk. I don't think that many of the House and Senate or [other] state officials would do that, but, sure, they know who contributed to their fundraisers. They know who their contributors were, and there is no doubt that a contributor to an officeholder expects, and the officeholder concurs, that [contributing] person has some status for contact. No doubt. Anybody who says, 'I don't arrange my schedule...I don't return calls to my family...or to folks I don't know, or folks I never heard of before, or to people who gave money to my opponent over folks who contributed to my campaign' — anybody who says that is not telling the truth. So, campaign contributions do...I don't say buy, but they do provide assurance of better access.

Former Senator Bob McFarland:

"Sure. Positively. Absolutely. Anybody who says it [contributions don't buy access] doesn't understand politics."

AMK: How close is it to buying? Did you ever witness, or feel like you were coming close to witnessing, a vote being swayed by money?

McFarland: No. Fortunately, one of the best laws we have on the books is that you can't make contributions during a [legislative] session. No, I don't think campaign contributions necessarily influence votes; I think they influence access for contact relative to an issue. But, if the Texas Medical Association gave me $25,000, they probably gave me that money because they felt I was going to be more attuned to their issue. [As a lobbyist] I don't make contributions to candidates that I don't think will ever see eye-to-eye with me and my clients on the issues. I don't think I'm buying anything, but I know their position. I think that's where most of these contributions are made. What you are seeing more and more of, too, is hedging bets, giving to both sides. That gets expensive, and it covers your ass. As Walter Mischer [a politically active Houston business leader] once said, 'You can always buy a ticket on the [winning candidate's] late train. It's just going to cost a lot more.' All of this is why you make contributions and how you make contributions. The system isn't going to change; it's going to cost more and more to finance campaigns, and most officeholders aren't independently wealthy.

But, is it getting too expensive, and are the contribution expectations becoming higher, higher and higher? I think the answer there is a definite yes. If an officeholder says there ought to be spending limits, he's going to be immediately criticized because he holds the office and has the name identification. He's doing that to thwart and frustrate any potential opponent. And when the lobby says, 'You've got to have limits on this thing,' they are criticized —'You're just saying that because you don't want to spend as much...you haven't been successful raising funds from your membership.' Sour grapes is all that is. Then you have the historic party situation, where the Republicans had a hue and cry for spending limits, and then they start electing members. And now that they are getting close to a majority, they're saying, 'We don't want any spending limits now.' The only force working against it...I don't think the public generally realizes what the cost of campaigns is. I'll bet not one out of a hundred voters have ever seen their [own legislator's] officeholder's campaign finance report. I don't think they care.

AMK: You see the cost of campaigning going up, yet you see voter apathy. Does it follow that voters are tuning out? Does it follow that way-too-expensive campaigns are the cause?

McFarland: I don't think so. I don't think it's the cost of campaigning or the amount of campaigning. That may turn a voter off in the sense that — 'Damn, it's another campaign season,' but I don't think that voter was inclined to vote, anyway. I think the campaign finance issue and the cost of campaigning is probably something that someone has set up in the political process of [explaining] why. I don't think it's a cause of voter apathy. I think the way the money is used probably turns people off. I think it's the trend of negative campaigning that's turning people off. If I see [Gov. George] Bush every night telling me 'what a sorry so and so' Al Gore is, that would turn voters off. Just seeing Bush on the TV every night isn't what does it. Part of the problem is that — 'if the other side is going to do it, we've got to do it.' I think that characterizes the flavor of the campaigning, and that may have more impact on apathy.

★   ★   ★

Interview with Paul Ragsdale, a former Democratic House member from Dallas, who is now a researcher in East Texas.

Anne Marie Kilday: What does the data on the 1998 elections — notably the total of $121 million, half coming from fewer than 700 donors — say about campaign finance in Texas?

Ragsdale: Well, the very elite are financing political campaigns. There are a very elitist few, running government. It is apparent that they have an inordinate amount of influence — the very elite — with these officials once they get elected, money talks. There is no way that a politician is going to deny these people access. And what's left over in Texas—what's left over goes into their officeholder accounts to finance all their [political] bills that the government doesn't finance.

AMK: And there's a trend lately of using officeholder accounts for contributions to other candidates?

Ragsdale: Yes, I've seen that here in local state races. When I was there [in the House], I used mine for charitable projects and my East Texas project, which was meant to empower black folks.

AMK: Does this kind of money lead to voter apathy?

Ragsdale: Of course it does. In this area here, folks just won't vote. The poverty level is higher. Many of them don't need a reason; they just figure their vote doesn't count. Apathy was rampant when I got elected, and it's way worse [now] than it was then. Now, it's like, 'Why should I vote, my vote doesn't count, anyway.' And when they see these [campaign contribution] numbers, they'll feel, 'Even if I do vote, it doesn't count, anyway. They [elected officials] aren't going to talk to me — they've got their own people they're going to talk to.' And that money is a dadgum big factor, I know myself. I would talk to people, trying to balance interests, but I don't think that there's much effort now in balancing interests. It's simply — 'my side or your side.'

AMK: When you were in the Legislature, did you ever witness that money equals a vote?

Ragsdale: I didn't witness it to my recollection, but I think it was there. Nobody was going to let you witness it. Bob Johnson [the late House Parliamentarian] used to call me the conscience of the House, so nobody was going to let me witness it. When I first went down there in 1973, I went to look at the composite photo of the House. That was the reform session after Sharpstown [the banking and stock-fraud scandal]...and the majority of the House were freshmen, so we started off with campaign finance, sunshine in government acts, like open meetings and open records. We were trying to get that taint out of state government.

Former Rep. Paul Ragsdale:

"They [big contributors] are very, very influential. And the public be damned. The contributors have undue influence, and I think that's bad. Now, if you call up with a personal problem, which is called constituent work, they'll get around to that eventually; but when it comes to public policy, having an influence there, you can forget that — that belongs to the contributors."

AMK: Did you feel it succeeded?

Ragsdale: It succeeded, for a while, but money is still going to run things. We obviously had some influence.

AMK: Did you have high hopes that the reforms would really clean up government?

Ragsdale: Well, at that time, we did, but everything is transitory. After a while folks figured out a way around it.

AMK: If you could design a reform plan today, would you put the same limits they have in the federal system [a contribution limit of $1,000 from individuals and $5,000 from PACs]?

Ragsdale: I don't know much about the federal system, but there ought to be some limits. I don't know that it would be $1,000. I think that, with the gross amounts being contributed, there ought to be some limits at the state level. We ought to exercise some judgement. There's a certain level where everybody ought to be able [to afford] to run for office.

AMK: What's driving up the cost of campaigning?

Ragsdale: The money is. The costs of campaigns have gone up, but the people who contribute drive it up, and the people who run for office drive it up.

AMK: So, do you think these contributors have access to public officials that the average citizen does not have?

Ragsdale: They are very, very influential. And the public be damned. The contributors have undue influence, and I think that's bad. Now, if you call up with a personal problem, which is called constituent work, they'll get around to that eventually; but when it comes to public policy, having an influence there, you can forget that—that belongs to the contributors.

★   ★   ★

Transcript of interview with Alec Rhodes, former Democratic House member from Dripping Springs, and businessman.

Anne Marie Kilday: Should there be limits on campaign contributions?

Rhodes: I think money is increasingly a factor all over, I really do. I think that no single step will solve the process; I think it's going to take improvement efforts that are coordinated. I think soft money is an important part of this; I think soft money is easily abused and it is hard to trace, so it is hard to have the responsibility go to the government. You asked me if money played a factor in my last race. I actually spent more money in my last race, in a losing effort, than I did in the previous two by a long shot. I spent lots more money, but part of it was that lots of the money that was spent [against me] never appeared on any Ethics report. Which, of course, doesn't affect a campaign whatsoever, but he was denying that he did these things. And they were slamming negative advertisements coming out of Dallas, and there was GOPAC out of Washington that was negative advertisement. He was saying he wasn't spending that much money and that kind of thing, so there was a distorted view. And, in a district like [House District] 46, which is predominantly small-town and rural, you don't have newspapers that have the time and the sophistication to unravel that sort of thing. So, there was not only did they not have time to look at the source of the negative advertising and where it was coming from, they didn't have time to figure out his report [or to] figure out if any of his allegations were true.

AMK: Sure, they just don't have that many people.

Rhodes: And, for example, the race didn't swing on this one issue. [Republican candidate, now-Rep. Rick] Green, in running against me, people accused him and documented on a number of times that he had not paid franchise taxes at the state level — he had a number of small businesses and it appeared that there was a pattern of him just not paying taxes on those things. When he was questioned on those things, he would jump and say, 'Well, Alec Rhodes didn't pay his taxes, either.' And the press, primarily in small towns, they're busy and they didn't have the time, so they

would just report it without investigating. Or, it would show up in campaign literature. And the fact of the matter was…this was not about campaign finance, it just was-
n't true. But you know, if you have the money you can spend your advertising dollars
where you want to, and if you are on a limited budget you've got to be choosy. They
talked about sticking to the message and that kind of thing. More dollars means more
message, and in a district like 46 it's very expensive to get the word to the voters. Far
more expensive than the voters realize. In listening to [former Democratic U.S. Sen.]
Paul Simon, I think where he is right, is that some of the problem would be solved if
you had public financing and you had equal access to the media and the means to say
it yourself.

In a district like 46, this is not a television district; this is a direct-mail district. In
fact, you've got a couple of different TV markets and you've got a couple of major
newspapers — the Austin Statesman and the San Antonio Express — and then there
are more than a handful of small-town newspapers. People are getting most of the
political information they get through direct mail. Well, direct mailing in an election
will cost you $12,000 to $14,000. I was always careful. I always had very nice looking
literature, and I had won a couple of campaigns. But Green had this four-color stuff,
lots of stuff, and he was just raining literature out here. Yes, [money] makes a difference. I was the incumbent and I had more of the lobby money than he did. I think I
probably spent $260,000 or $270,000 [on a House race], and he spent about
$350,000, so he spent about $80,000 more. He had regular television advertisement
and people were in shock when we had to come up with, I think it was $70,000, to
go up on television. And, of course, you're only getting part of the market. There is
no question that money affects your ability to get word to the voters. He was able to
spend television money for a positive message and mail money for a negative message, so he was able to do both things. I'll be frank with you, those things did not win
the election for him, but they made a difference.

AMK: That district is changing with all the newcomers coming in?
Rhodes: Very much. Well, here's the deal: There were something like 8,000 new voters in the last election. The people who are coming in from other parts of the country, they are these electronic business folks and the politics are different [from where
they came]. Furthermore, you can be a conservative and be a Democrat in Texas, and

they come here and they are used to thinking Republican. People in Dripping Springs depend on the local papers to get news of the county commissioners. It's a very split market. There are people who vote here who don't even know they live in Hays County. They watch the news on television that's Austin news. They go to work in Austin. Their community is their kids and their churches, so they don't even know local politics. When they vote, they vote how they used to vote — they vote Republican. Now, some of them will change over time...[as] they come out here and start voting Republican and realize that somebody else will drink the water out from under them, or pollute that water. So then, they begin to take some interest in issues that traditionally are championed by Democrats. And, people out here are big supporters of public education. And I will tell you — I was in the Legislature — people who support public education are Democrats, not Republicans. So, I will say that as people begin to understand some of these issues they become more open-minded, but it's not when they are first here. I will also say that the media is such that people form their opinions based on advertising. The fact is that only people who are politicians read all that [political direct mail] crap. Everyday folks don't necessarily know who their [state] representative is, or their county judge, or even their county commissioner. Most people live a life, they take kids to football, they go to PTA and church. They don't live their lives around politicians. So what happens is when the time comes for an election, here comes all this literature, and you see the headlines on it on the way to the trash can. They don't even read all of it. It makes a lot of difference. And of course, Green was identifying himself with Bush. All those kinds of things played into it, but that ability to have both positive and negative images...was helped by money.

AMK: What position did money play in the Legislature's decision-making?

Rhodes: I think that money played and continues to play an increasing part, primarily because of the high cost of getting the [campaign] message out to the voters. In some districts, there were members who could go to their constituents and get some good amounts of money, but in Hays, Caldwell and Gonzales counties there's a lot of poor folks. While I got a broad base of support, a lot of $10 to $25 contributions, it takes a ton of those to get to $250,000. I depended on the lobby trying to hold that seat.

Former Rep. Alec Rhodes:

"I saw people, and I'm not going to mention names here, who obviously got a pile of money from insurance companies [and] who carried the water for the insurance folks [in the Legislature]. I saw people who got a lot of money from the Chemical Council and people like that, who [then] opposed environmental protection. Things I thought we really needed."

AMK: Some research has shown that 80 percent of every campaign dollar is from outside the average legislator's district?

Rhodes: I'd be surprised if it wasn't higher than that. If you're in office, if you're the incumbent, you are in a position where you've got to go back again and again for the money. Personally, I did a pretty good job, I thought. I got to the point with at least one group, where I'm sure I could have gotten more money, but I didn't feel comfortable asking for more money. The process of asking... forces you to spend a lot of time with the people who give you money. I think there is a human tendency...people like to say what other folks want to hear. That may just be my politician speaking, but it's hard to be controversial when you are trying to fight them for money. Furthermore, I think the smart lobbyists, they don't give huge amounts...to a state rep's race. In my races, you get $250 or $500 every election cycle. That means that many times, just because you're forced to be doing that, you get to know those people. I also believe that as in other parts of life: 5 percent of the people are outstanding at what they do, 5 percent ought to be in jail, and the other 90 percent are trying to do it in ways that aren't all good.... There were a lot of people who would never give me money, because they knew that I wasn't ever going to vote for them. There were certain lobbyists that didn't want to see me coming; I never had the clout for them [to give]. So, you have the people that helped you [in a campaign]. And, when you are making decisions at the legislative level and you have some kind of relationship with those people, if they are good at articulating their point — you know, information is power — and if they are good at articulating their points well, they are persuasive. They are friendly, they've helped you [in the past]. And I think that was true. I saw people, and I'm not going to mention names here, who obviously got a pile of money from insurance companies [and] who carried the water for the insurance folks [in the Legislature]. I saw people who got a lot of money from the Chemical Council and people like that, who [then] opposed environmental protection. Things I thought we really needed. And I think that was a product of that. Frankly, committee chairmen, who've got a lot of power, also got more donations from those folks.

I think there is no question that at the federal and at the state level, money talks. I got to the point where I got along with the people at Southwestern Bell. But, I [also] got to the point where I was not going to ask them for any more money. I did not want to be in that position...and I felt I was still pretty independent. I took money from Philip Morris, and I own stock in Philip Morris. I never one time voted for the tobacco industry. I never had any Philip Morris lobbyist come to me for a thing. It's far more common when you have big contributions. Another thing is a lot of folks who give money were giving money based on the fact that they knew I tried to be open-minded. I voted for a lot of tort-reform things, yet I received a lot of money from the trial lawyers. Looking back now, I'm not sure I agree with all of my votes; I know there are a few I don't agree with. A lot of it was when I got in the Legislature and I was learning. The pressure is enormous, you have a dearth of information, and it takes you a while to [get] where you understand the behind-the-scenes stuff. You are desperate for information. And, a lot of people are terrible at telling their own story; the lobbyists are better at it. My real strength in the Legislature was that I was a real good committee member, and I was good at eliciting information from people who weren't themselves doing a good job of telling their side of the story. That's what I liked to do. So I really worked at bringing the other side out. When you need information, in general, you go to a lobbyist, because a lobbyist, in general, is better at telling their story, since they stay there year after year; and they know enough to tell you some of both sides. Now a bunch of lobbyists, if they were all on one side, I knew I was on the other — automatically. But in summary, money greases that, and in those races money is important in getting the word out. Newspapers do a bad job of political reporting — in talking about the dynamics, in reporting on the issues, and who is on which side; about people on this side are opposed to the people on that side. And, because of television, because of sound bites, because news has been turned into entertainment — we don't really have an appetite for that type of political analysis in our news writing. They don't know how to ask the questions.... I can't say I'm a great fan. But, then you go to those small-town newspapers. Hell, what a life! You give them a story and you can get it in there, but I couldn't even get public service announcements in Republican papers.

★ ★ ★

Transcript of interview with A.R [Babe] Schwartz, a former Democratic House member and state Senator from Galveston, and now a lobbyist.

Anne Marie Kilday: Let's talk about campaign fundraising excesses...

Schwartz: [First, he said a two-inch-thick stack of notices about legislative fundraisers was waiting in his office when he returned from a month-long absence; many of the two-hour parties at the Austin Club were for House and Senate candidates who had no primary or general-election opponents.] I really think the gross amounts of money being spent are because the public-relations people and the media hounds have done a great job of convincing the people who run for office that the amount of money you spend directly reflects on whether you will win or not. So, you have to raise all the money you can, and spend every bit of it. They start spending for public consumption: Television, number one; newspapers, number two, dailies and then the weeklies; and in today's climate, radio. Now suppose you're running for state representative in Galveston County — you buy television in Houston to reach a market of 400,000 or more [homes], the same as a Houston candidate, but [the Galveston candidate] can only reach 100,000 people [in his district], and 25,000 of them might vote. So the truth is, you are spending the same amount of money as a candidate for the U.S. Senate, and the cost is the same. How can a state representative get elected when he's got to do that? If you're in Galveston County and you buy a newspaper ad, the island reads the Galveston News. The mainland [part of Galveston County] reads the Texas City Sun and the Houston Chronicle. That's the cost factor. Buying television just isn't worth the money.

The consultants are saying, 'You've got to do this. You can't feel safe about this [campaign] unless you do this.' And, of course, the consultants get [a commission of] 15 percent of [the cost of] placing the ads. And billboards, if you have any money left over, you buy those. And, what it's all about is, it sells the lobby. If you do all that, then the Austin lobby takes notice and starts saying, 'This guy is going to clean house.' I think the consultants have sold this deal to everybody who runs for office and they've done a real good job of it. The amounts of money being spent are horrendous.

AMK: What impact does all that advertising have on the average voter?

Schwartz: Well, I've always been told that the average literacy rate is about eighth grade, so the consultants would say aim your advertising to them. I always felt that those people weren't voting anyway, so all these voter drives that the Democrats would conduct — aimed at these eighth-grade dropouts — wouldn't get out the vote. And they say aim the ads at the 18-to-25-year olds — and they don't vote either.

AMK: Why don't they vote?

Schwartz: It's the average mindset of everyone else, 'My vote doesn't really count.' And then, the younger voters haven't really gotten into the system yet. They're not even disenchanted with government; they're not involved in government. It's the older folks who can't get their welfare check on time or their Medicare, the older people who have been abused by government sufficiently — they're apt to be voters because they feel they've been abused by government. The 18-to-25-year olds don't have any contact with government, so they don't care about government. I used to make a speech talking about how I ran for office while I was still in law school. My theory is, that is what a young politician ought to do before they get jaundiced. But luckily, I lost that election. I had worked, been in the Navy, and I was in law school. I didn't have any experience in government, so I would have sat somewhere in the House of Representatives trying to figure out what everybody was talking about. It seems to me that there's not much you can appeal to an 18-to-25-year old about that will involve them in government.

Former Senator Babe Schwartz:

"That office (Railroad Commission) is worth nothing to anybody but the oil and gas industry, as it used to be to the trucking business. You build your campaign base there."

AMK: Why is there such voter apathy? Is the spending a factor? Do the voters think the special interests are in charge?

Schwartz: You may be right. Unless they are part of a group that has an agenda for change, then they don't know why they're voting...what it is that they want. Suppose they sit around and think about it: Am I trying to impose a philosophy on government? Do I care whether they are Republican or Democrat? Or, do I like this person? Most of the time, that's based on — 'All I really know about this person is what I've seen on television or in the newspaper.' If they really sat and analyzed it, voters might realize they're voting for a person simply because of advertising. The truth is, we know damn little about the people we vote for, and advertising is aimed at getting your vote, based on personal appeal, rather than merit, because merit doesn't sell. [Former Democratic Gov.] Ann Richards, in the first interview after losing the campaign to [Republican George W.] Bush, said the lesson she had learned was that she had kept telling people what she had done for them, but she didn't tell them what she was going to do for them.

I think I felt most of the time in my campaigns that everything I paid money for was lousy. In the end, people thought about the image and record I had over that 20 years. They identified me with working people and their status in life. Also, I convinced them in my advertising that I worked hard and I produced. In Galveston, I pointed to what money I brought home — the UT medical branch and Texas A&M at Clear Lake. It took me a long time to get that impression across; instead, of [being seen as] the wild-eyed liberal and almost a communist.

AMK: Do you think voters are aware of the enormous contributions?
Schwartz: The average voter doesn't have any idea about a guy named [Dick] Weekley, who is a real-estate developer and who, in this new era of tort reform, gives $100,000 to a state senator. Hell, that state senator doesn't have a vote anymore— Weekley has a vote.

AMK: You really believe that?
Schwartz: Ain't no question about it. Anybody who accepts $100,000 from a PAC belongs, body and soul, to that PAC. And I would defy anybody to find me a vote, for any motion or committee action, where that person wasn't a slave to that $100,000 contribution.

AMK: When you were in the Legislature, did you ever see votes get sold?

Schwartz: I don't think so. I wouldn't characterize it as being sold. I certainly believe that campaign contributions were the single most important factor [in legislative voting]. But those people [legislators] would say, 'I got those contributions because they know I'm for them, so they just support me.' And there's a lot of truth to that, but I tell you what it does is, it guarantees it. Trying to persuade somebody to vote against them is an insurmountable task. I can remember a speech I made on a trucking bill...against the truckers...I remember I was pounding on my desk...here goes this 18-wheeler, boom, boom, boom. And then, you hit the potholes. And I said, in that speech, 'If God Himself or Herself came down from the heavens and begged you to vote not to do this, this bill would still get 30 votes in the Texas Senate.' And the bill got 30 votes. I was the only vote against it. I could talk about truckers...and the Railroad Commission — hell, there hasn't been an independent vote on the Railroad Commission since I first took public office; because, the oil and gas industry, the people who are supposed to be regulated, give plenty of money to Railroad Commission races. I railed about the Railroad Commission for 20 years in the Senate. And the only thing you can say positive about the Railroad Commission is that it's a place for people to gain a little notoriety, so they can run for some other public office. That office is worth nothing to anybody but the oil and gas business, as it used to be [to] the trucking business. You build your campaign contribution base there. It's interesting to me that the Public Utility Commission, because it's appointed, is not that way. They didn't take money to get there, so they are not politically aligned in our system. Without that money, you don't have the status to get elected. If we had an elected PUC, they'd be running for office just like the Railroad Commissioners. They'd have the money, too.

AMK: Do you think that the demise of the two-newspaper towns in Texas has contributed to voter apathy?

Schwartz: I think that's true. Muckraking is wonderful for politics. There's nobody that's going to scoop you if you haven't got any competition. I really have seen in my lifetime the evolution [from] the ability to get elected to public office without a great deal of money. When I got elected, I was really a good state representative. Now, I'm saying it's the worst of times in public finance. The Austin American-Statesman essentially bullied the Legislature into passing that ethics bill. The members saw the Statesman pounding on them about ethics, so they passed a silly ethics bill that requires people to do a bunch of silly stuff, like to go through this stupidity of filing a [lobbyist's] report on the 10th of the month to tell how much you spent taking people to dinner. And, it's being violated every day. You can give them $100,000 [in campaign contributions] to pay for all the golf they want...but you're not supposed to spend more than $50 per day on a member [as a lobbyist].

AMK: Did that put more emphasis on the campaign check?

Schwartz: It didn't change anything. It's still being done. If you want to take a [legislator] golfer for the $75 green fees, you just split it between two lobbyists. You can each spend less than $50 per day. I report my entertainment, and I enjoy my entertainment, but failure to do so just results in a $100 fine. Big deal. I know there's golf every day; there's fishing every day; and it would be very easy for one lobbyist to exceed his $250 limit every day at just a legislative conference. When I was in the House, in 1957, Stone [Red] Wells was the lobbyist for Tennessee Gas, and a Tennessee Gas plane took a group of legislators to the Kentucky Derby. Well, during that session, there was a proposal to raise the tax on natural gas. While they were gone we got the bill up, so the gas [lobby] boys had to chub it [delay the bill by debating it excessively] until they got the plane back. The press corps was waiting for them at the airport, but the pilots got word of that, so they went to someplace else — San Marcos or Georgetown — and had cars waiting for them and herded 'em all back to Austin. When they got back into the House, we were all chanting, 'We know where you've been! We know where you've been!' [He then recalled other weekly "freebies" from lobby groups, including the weekly fish fry sponsored by the beer lobby and the barbecue sponsored by the trial lawyers.]

The ethics bill stopped that to some degree. Well, the same amount of money is being spent; it's just being spent differently. It gives the appearance of shifting the money, and it shifts some money, but I don't think it reduces the amount of money that is being spent.

AMK: What do you really think should be done in the way of reforming the Texas campaign-finance system?

PERSPECTIVES FROM THE PLAYERS

Schwartz: I really feel that we have to address the issue of how campaign funds are spent. And, I think we absolutely have to address the issue of how campaign funds must be terminated after the defeat of a candidate. Period. Set it out in statute. My goal would be for that money to go into the general fund. There is no rhyme or reason for Bill Hobby to have a fund, and there was no reason for [the late Bob] Bullock to have a fund. It [campaign funds] should have to terminate. And, while you are collecting money, you shouldn't be allowed to collect any money if you don't have a primary opponent. Then there should be a date set for you to raise money for the general election. So, there ought to be cut-off dates, because that money is still being used for personal purposes — like house payments, condominium payments, airplanes. I don't know how many things go into that. I don't know what the statute says. I do know there are pretty liberal interpretations of what you can spend that money for. All we're doing is making contributions to people who enhance their own relationships with that money. A lot of it still goes to personal use. I think it's still permissible, but the real problem is, it can continue to be raised incessantly. Even after you leave office, if you've got half a million dollars [in an old campaign account], you're making a lot of money. The real campaign reformers have hopes to limit money that goes into campaigns, or eliminate soft money. Instead of trying to limit, or [eliminate] soft money, the reporting system has to be better and it has to be clear.

There ought to be a clear identity, with the name of the PAC and the purpose of the PAC stated. That way, if Weekley [of Texans for Lawsuit Reform] gives $5,000 to a state senator...really, the public ought to have an easy way to know whom the guy sold out to. We're talking about big money. When I refer to selling out, I'm talking about $50,000 or $100,000. You don't get that kind of money because of your reputation. I had a $2,500 limit on individuals, and a $7,500 limit from PACs, the trial lawyers and the AFL-CIO. Toward the end of the campaign in 1980, when I had a tough race, Perry Bass [of the Fort Worth oil family] said he wanted to give more and so did [Houston oil and real-estate investor] George Mitchell. I said, 'You've already given me $2,500.' I said I didn't want any more money; I had spent all of the money I was going to spend. I could have simply said I really needed $25,000, but it seemed stupid. There are people who say when you lose your luster you do things like that, but I really didn't think I was going to lose. After the campaign, I wrote Mitchell a thank-you letter for his contribution, and Mitchell sent me another $2,500. I had to call him and say, 'George, read your mail!'

Office-holder accounts have been the ruination of a good system, but keep this in mind, legislators don't earn any money [in that job]. By 1967, after I had a few good [law] clients, I could have stayed in the Legislature all my life. And now my retirement is so good, I'm embarrassed about it. When [former Bryan Sen.] Bill Moore got that [legislative] retirement tied to the salaries of district judges, he threatened to exclude me…so I just went and got myself a cup of coffee and the bill passed.

8

"Anybody who accepts $100,000 from a PAC
belongs body and soul to that PAC.
And I would defy anybody to find me a vote, for any
motion or committee action, to show that that person
wasn't a slave to that $100,000 contribution."

— From A.R. (Babe) Schwartz, former House and Senate member, and now lobbyist

★   ★   ★

WHERE DO WE GO FROM HERE?

As noted at the outset, Texas campaign-finance reporting law hasn't changed much since it was adopted in 1973. It's been tweaked, along with the ethics and lobby-regulation laws, to be sure, but only in response to news media coverage that highlights specific problems. That's just the news media doing their jobs, of course, but politicians sometimes react before scandal truly attaches. For example: East Texas poultry magnate Lonnie (Bo) Pilgrim was caught handing out $10,000 checks to Texas senators (but blank as to payee) on the Senate floor, while an issue that he was interested in was being discussed in committee. The Legislature's response? It changed the law to make it illegal to accept a campaign gift in the Capitol building. A separate change in the law made it illegal to collect campaign money just before, during and just after a legislative session, the theory being that actual lawmaking should appear to be disconnected from the fund-raising process. And, after a series of Austin American-Statesman stories on elaborate lobby-financed legislative entertainment, and golf, hunting, fishing, and ski trips, the Legislature clamped down on itself by outlawing pure junkets and cutting down on legislators' acceptance of free meals and expensive gifts. As you read in the interviews that came before, some political players feel that single change in the law alone added to the escalation in the size of campaign donations. The Legislature also enacted limits on how much of their personal loans candidates for statewide executive-branch offices could reimburse themselves from campaign money. But the law gave enough wiggle room so that a wealthy candidate, rather than making personal loans to his own campaign, can guarantee bank loans to the campaign and not be limited in his subsequent reimbursement from campaign funds. Plus, the Ethics Commission was created in 1991 as a purported watch dog over the campaign-finance and ethics laws — although its toothlessness is widely conceded, if not secretly celebrated, by state officials.

* * *

So there are a couple of truths that need to be adopted before proceeding: a) Something has to be demonstrably wrong, and broadly condemned by the voters, in order to generate reforms by a Legislature that is itself at the center of a problem. And, b) "Reform" doesn't always do what was intended, although it's hard to imagine making Texas' current campaign-finance law worse. If in doubt of the law of unintended consequences, check out the state of Washington, which by a 1992 voter-proposed initiative adopted a variety of approaches to reducing the influence of "special interest" contributions and opening up the electoral process. In the subsequent three election cycles, however, Washington voters have seen how ineffective the initiative was: Special-interest money flows more freely; incumbents raise as much or more money, and win as often as before; high-dollar givers have increased; business-related PACs give only a slightly lower percentage of total dollars; and far more money is now spent on "independent expenditures" for which there is little public reporting. Note that this was a voter initiative, over which the Washington legislators had no control; but also note that they haven't done anything statutorily to improve on the initiative.

In Washington or Texas, what the National Institute on Money in State Politics calls the "cash constituents" of elected officials are a major factor. Those are the so-called special interests and other large individual contributors who have ongoing influence in the policy process. And they are the same givers who keep the election machinery greased with friction-free cash for elections and even, as some of the preceding interviews also reveal, for the favorite causes of incumbent politicians. It is not a leap of logic to believe that the ordinary voter feels that the "cash constituents" have a disproportionate role in passing and killing legislation. Yet, as noted at the end of Chapter 6, one sample of big-money donors and voters shows that while not always on the same page about other issues, they agree on that disproportionate role.

* * *

There's at least a rebuttable presumption that campaign money speaks from those who give it, and to those who get it. That's particularly true for an incumbent who seeks re-election. Those who have been best served by his tenure would be best served again, right? And no less a source than the U.S. Supreme Court, in its 1976 Buckley vs. Valeo decision upholding campaign contribution limits, held that Congress recognized a "compelling interest" in safeguarding against the "appearance of corruption spawned by the real or imagined coercive influence of large financial contributions." Plus, in January, 2000, the U.S. Supreme Court, in a case out of Missouri, reaffirmed the power of states to set low contribution limits. States may set limits as low as they see fit so long as the limits are not "so radical in effect as to render political association ineffective, drive the sound of a candidate's voice below the level of notice and render contributions pointless."

So there's no question that contribution limits can be enacted, as in fact they have been. A huge majority of the other states (36) has enacted contribution limits in state and/or local campaigns, which so far have survived challenge in federal court. (Voter-initiative-imposed donor limits in California and Oregon, which would be the 37th and 38th states with state contribution limits, were still on appeal at this writing.) Some home-rule cities in Texas have adopted their own version of restrictions on campaign finance, though none so drastic as Austin's individual contribution limit of $100. The Texas House has voted several times in favor of limits on contributions in state campaigns, and, as we noted in Chapter 2, there already is a Texas limit on contributions in judicial races.

The key issue for legislators, here and elsewhere, is if there are to be caps, what is a reasonable limit on contributions? For nearly three decades, the federal limit has been $1,000 per election for individuals (that is, $1,000 each for a primary, a run-off and a general election) and $5,000 per election for political action committees. The federal government also has an individual aggregate limit of $25,000 on total contributions to U.S. Senate and House candidates in an election cycle, though that limit doesn't apply to PACs and is rarely enforced against individuals. (Plus, in federal campaigns the two parties have their own unlimited "soft money" accounts, which supposedly are only to be spent for party-building programs, but which, in truth, are routinely spent to identify party-building in terms of a party candidate's stand on issues.)Whatever is done about limits on campaign contributions, if anything, the amounts should not be set in stone, but indexed to inflation, such as the Consumer Price Index. If anyone tries to tell you that $1,000 in politics buys as much today as it did in 1975, ask that same person if he could buy the same amount of groceries for $1,000 today as he did in 1975. Granted, politicians don't shop for political talent or advertising at the supermarket, but their dollars depreciate the same as anyone else's.

★ ★ ★

For anyone, a cap on campaign contributions is the biggest hurdle in any talk about campaign-finance reform. Indeed, when you bring up the subject with political players, most will instantly shift the focus to what they perceive as "full disclosure" of who is getting how much from whom and, correlatively, who is spending how much on which expenses. The goal in any new law should be to make the campaign-finance disclosure process transparent, not opaque as it is now. The Legislature never has enacted full disclosure, of course, but already it's easier to see who is financing Texas statewide executive-branch and legislative candidates, thanks to the 1999 law mentioned at the top of this chapter. That's because it's on the Internet (to get at it, go to www.ethics.state.tx.us), though the Legislature decided (inexcusably, in my mind) to put it there without the street addresses of donors. That's a simple thing to change, as well as to put all other politics-related reports in searchable form on the Internet — most obviously the lobby disclosure forms.

Hands-down easy, too, is another big fix: Require all candidates to list all donors with their occupation or principal field of endeavor, their employer or the firm with which they are associated and the address of that business. Listing occupation and employer is crucial to knowing the economic interests backing a candidate, which inexplicably is why making that information public has been rejected by the Legislature in the past. The federal government's reports for presidential, senatorial and congressional candidates already require that information. So does the separate statute on Texas judicial candidates. Also, it is always requested of contributors to both major parties, and to all candidates with reasonably sophisticated money-raising systems. Plus, once in office, all public officials want (some say need) to know who gave them how much and when; the odds are good they will run for office again, and that is a ready-made shopping list. Once more, the officeholder keeps that information in his own political data bank; the voter should be able to know the same things.

More solid recommendations on campaign-finance reporting:

• Require that each candidate file a single report, through which all money is reported, even if it's from a PAC that spends its own money to help that candidate only and that also has to file its own report. If a party committee or a PAC supporting a slate of candidates (such as Blue-eyed Left-handed Democrats East of the Colorado PAC) spends money on its own, it must allocate a benefit to each candidate and report that benefit amount to each candidate, as well as to the Ethics Commission. So-called conduit reporting would eliminate some big-money shell games.

• Require candidates and political committees to itemize expenditures made by or through political and media consultants, fund-raisers, pollsters, etc. Remember, these reports on how the money is spent are required on behalf of a well-informed public, and those who give money are entitled to be well-informed, too, about how the money is spent. If $50,000 pays a TV ad creator's fee, as well as the cost of buying time for the ad on a station, that information should be reported, not sheltered.

• If contributions are limited, require that loans from or guaranteed by someone other than the candidate be reported subject to the limits, as if they were direct contributions. Also, repeal the provision that lets a candidate be reimbursed for a bank loan to his campaign on which he is the guarantor. Instead, limit a candidate's personal reimbursement for all money out of their own pockets. This principle should be applied to the separate judicial-campaign reports, too.

• Make statewide candidates comply with the same last-minute contribution report requirement that legislative candidates face. This report should be extended to all judicial candidates as well.

• Require statewide and legislative candidates to list cash on hand on every report, including the end-of-campaign report, and include loans outstanding and bills still unpaid. This is an issue of public trust, though similar to a borrower's financial statement to a bank. And judicial candidates have to do roughly the same thing in their separate statute.

• Most other large and politically aware states require that out-of-state PACs report on their own, the same as in-state PACs, who contributed to the PAC and who in Texas got the PAC's money. Now they skate the law by simply filing a copy of their federal registration statement.

• It's reasonable, even if it would be controversial, to limit by percentage or amount of a legislative candidate's contributions from outside that candidate's district. There would be attempts to circumvent the law, perhaps, but those attempts would be newsworthy, too. In Alaska, it's illegal for a registered lobbyist to contribute to a legislative candidate if the lobbyist doesn't live in that candidate's district.

★   ★   ★

Experts and amateurs alike have recommended other reforms over the years. In 1988, Jack M. Rains of Houston, Gov. Bill Clements' secretary of state in his second term, proposed that anyone contributing more than $25,000 to all candidates for state offices in an election cycle has to report, on his own, how his money was distributed. Rains also proposed that anybody who does any kind of business with, or lobbies at a state agency headed by elected officials, must report any contributions he or his law firm, or company or a PAC made to the decision-makers. The Texas Senate passed those provisions as part of a larger bill in 1989 that then died in the House. Another idea is that there should be a limit on how much good government anyone should be able to buy: Over the years, reformers have proposed a $25,000 or $50,000 aggregate limit on how much an individual Texan can give to all statewide and legislative candidates. As mentioned earlier, the federal aggregate limit is $25,000 per election cycle to all U.S. Senate and U.S. House candidates.

Under current law, a one-time candidate or a long-time officeholder can maintain a political account consisting of retained, but unspent, political contributions. The so-called "tail" goes on forever if the person keeps a campaign treasurer on file or has not filed a "final report." That practice should be ended, so that donations, assets bought with contributions, and interest or other income are disposed of within six years after the person ceases to be a candidate or after the date of the election in which he was last a candidate. (A whip to ensure that the left-over money is given to other politicians or parties or to higher education, for example, would be a law saying that six years after a candidate loses or leaves office, his left-over funds escheat to the state.) The squishiness in the current law allows former big shots to keep calling the shots by giving out campaign contributions as long as the money lasts.

Everybody won't agree that a "truth-in-naming" law needs to be passed. State law now requires that the name of a general-purpose PAC, which might give to statewide as well as judicial and legislative candidates, must reflect the name of a corporation, labor union or other association or legal entity "other than an individual" that controls the PAC. That may be as precise as the law can get, but it ain't much. Anyone can argue about what is the most misleading name on the PAC list at any given time.

But, under current law, you might never know that a mythical group called Texans for Control of Pollution, say, was the PAC of giant water-pollution permit holders in the petrochemical industry. Or, that an equally mythical PAC called Texas Committee to Improve the Judiciary, say, was a group of plaintiffs' trial lawyers opposing merit appointment of judges.

★   ★   ★

Changes at the Texas Ethics Commission are a thread in every reformer's conversation, though the commission gets little attention among the news media and other political players. The fact is, it's been alive for nine years, but it doesn't have a reputation for doing much of anything. I referred earlier to its toothlessness almost casually, but that's because the agency isn't taken seriously by any of the 100 or so people I've talked to while doing this project. It also was an "instant fix" during House-Senate negotiations on the 1991 ethics bill, which as a whole was such a cut-and-paste operation that not until long after the conference report had become law did many people know its content. The agency also has not been through the Sunset review process yet, but is up for review in 2003. (The initial review was supposed to be in 2001, but it was postponed while Ethics set up and implemented the 1999 statute on Internet listing of the reports.) The quick version of its faults: It is mired in procedural red tape and squirrelly secrecy. The staff has never initiated a complaint or an investigation of its own, or even a limited-purpose random audit of campaign-finance reports. The commission, as of January, 2000, had never subpoenaed a witness or a document, never made a criminal referral, and never held a formal enforcement hearing. And nothing is open to the public, even the substance of a complaint, until or unless there is a formal enforcement hearing. The commission's toughest action yet is a fine of $5,000 (the maximum allowable) for a campaign-finance shell game against an arm of Houston Dr. Steven Hotze's political operation; it was still on appeal within the agency's procedures as of this writing. At the end of 1999, of the 145 orders the commission had issued, 85 carried no penalty at all or a $100 fine, which is peanuts and less than a slap on the wrist for most campaigns.

Executive director Tom Harrison, almost a career state campaign-law expert who has been in this job since 1995, says the commission's staff is limited in its authority: If a complaint is filed and the respondent says it's not true, the commission decides whether to act further. Most complaints die at that stage, in fact. And, despite the half-Republican, half-Democrat make-up of the commission, Harrison says, that initial decision isn't based on partisanship; in almost all cases, commission members don't even know the names of the parties. Harrison says the agency's "secrecy" reputation stems from the statute: The person who files a complaint, and the person against whom it is filed, can say all they want to in public about the case; but the agency isn't allowed to say anything — even to acknowledge that it has a complaint on file, or that it doesn't.

At a minimum, the Ethics Commission needs more personnel; it has 33 now, and was stretched to the limit during the computerization project for putting campaign finance on the Internet. The statute must allow the staff to initiate investigations independently, to conduct detailed audits of X percentage of all reports filed by category (statewide, legislative and judicial), and to find gaps in reporting and make recommendations for change to the commission, then to the Legislature. The commission itself should concentrate on broad policy issues, not decide on minutiae, like whether an investigation is worth opening based on a complaint. And a number of legislators say the law could be changed to simplify the complaint-handling process, too: Let the staff do the investigating, then hold a formal hearing if there's substance involved and use preponderance of the evidence rather than the "clear and convincing" evidentiary standard it uses now. Any change in the law should also make clear that the subpoena power of the agency means its staff can call witnesses and obtain documents rather than be limited to what the parties submit.

For the future, somebody has to get a handle on independent expenditures and issue advertising. That's all the fad in federal campaigns these days — proving the old adage that political money will always try to find a route to its purpose — and it's just a matter of time until Texas gets more of that semi-anonymous advertising than has been seen in the past. The law is the law, of course, but there has been no systematic policing or even watching. Again, it should be worth investigating during the Sunset process, if the law isn't updated in the meantime. Indeed, because it is itself now on-line for campaign-finance reports, perhaps the Ethics Commission should also be given broad-brush enforcement authority over the Internet part of political advertising. The Internet, with its hard-to-trace tentacles, is likely to increase in importance in the future, because it enables a candidate to remain message-positive in the other paid electronic media while being literally and wantonly negative in cyberspace. The potential for avoiding official, reportable campaign costs is what's most at issue.

★   ★   ★

Legislative pay raises have never had what you might call popular support, but conflict-of-interest laws always do. I combine them here for the simple reason that increasing one justifies tightening the other, and both of them need work. Texas pays its legislators $600 a month, or about $150 a week, and that was a big reform 40 years ago — up from $400 a month. We've always justified that pittance by saying we believe in the concept of citizen-legislators who convene in Austin for 140 days every two years but spend the rest of their time earning a living under the laws they pass. Yet five years ago a Public Citizen of Texas survey showed that Texas legislators work in excess of 60 hours a week while they're in session, and well more than that during the last month of a session, but even put in 20 hours a week on legislative work when they're not in session. (It turns out we citizens want these guys to "work 140 days every two years" — except when we, as constituents, have trouble with a state agency, and then we want help now!)

When they created the Ethics Commission in 1991, the legislators empowered that part-time board to recommend legislative pay raises subject only to voter approval, thus taking the Legislature out of the pay-raise picture. But the commission hasn't used that power, and won't do so until the speaker of the House and the lieutenant governor give their blessing in advance. One creative approach is to require, by statute, that at least once a decade the Ethics Commission take a pay-raise recommendation directly to the voters. That doesn't mean the voters would buy it, but at least they would know that the Legislature isn't trying to boost its own pay. We're at the bottom of the heap among states; even Oklahoma, tiny by economic or any other comparison except football, pays its part-time lawmakers more than five times as much as we do.

"Conflict of interest" is something like the obverse of pornography in the political world: One man's struggle to make a living is another's dirty book. Texas ranks sixth among the states in its ethics-law personal financial disclosure statement, according to a Center for Public Integrity study, but that may say more about other states' laws than it does about our own. The state constitution and ethics law require a legislator to disclose a business or professional interest that would directly benefit from proposed legislation unless the legislation affects an entire class of businesses, and prohibit a legislator from voting on that legislation. To let the public in on the potential conflict, a legislator (and a statewide official as well) must file a financial disclosure statement about his business and personal holdings. But the law was passed in 1973, and "over $25,000" is the top category for disclosure. At the very least, another couple of categories need to be added, say, "$25,000 to $100,000" and "over $100,000." Lawmakers also need to provide for enforcement of the requirement that legislators identify clients who have legislative interests. Even Rep. Pete Gallego, D-Alpine, a sponsor of some campaign-finance reforms, was embarrassed in 2000 when his legislative role was featured in his Austin-based law firm's Internet web pages — including his passage of a bill that was supported by a client of the law firm. (That happened, Gallego said, without his knowing that the firm worked on the legislation, much less that it lobbied the Legislature at all.) And a somewhat more difficult to enforce, though legitimate, reform proposal would say that no legislator can vote on an issue that affects 10 percent of his assets or 10 percent of his income or line of business.

* * *

Reformers don't forget, of course, their favorite foils — lobbyists. They want immediate reporting of lobby contracts, as well as more precise reporting of the subject matter and estimated cost of those contracts. That's not unreasonable, given the tight on-going financial relationships that many lobbyists have with legislators and the presumably non-financial relationships they have with agency officials whom they also lobby. Legislators shouldn't be feathering a future lobby nest for themselves, and the public interest isn't served by turning in your "SO" (for state official) license plate one day and hanging out a "hire me" shingle the next day. But I also know literally dozens of former lawmakers, both in Austin and in Washington, who are as honorable and honest in their lobby dealings as they were in their legislating days. Congress faced this great crisis of public confidence some years back, and its response was to prohibit direct person-to-person lobbying by former members for a year after leaving office. That might be a reasonable cooling-off period for Texas, too, as it normally would let a legislator complete his cushy $600-a-month job in peace and miss only one regular session before prospering as a lobbyist.

*   *   *

Also, though it has little legislative support in Texas at this point, some reformers always want to discuss public financing of campaigns for public office. To deal with the "nut" candidate issue, too, the supporters qualify it with some kind of threshold-of-support requirement, such as raising X amount of private money in small gifts or Y amount within a district, before public money would kick in. In Maine, candidates are eligible for public financing if they raise a number of $5 contributions and they agree to abide by a state-established limit on total spending. In New York City, public financing provides a 4 to 1 matching ratio for small contributions, so one $50 private hit multiplies to $250 in spendable cash. But there have only been a few experiments with public financing, none of them yet with a long track record, and none of them applying to statewide campaigns in a state with a large population. And the declining level of public participation in the federal income tax check-off program for presidential candidates may indicate that the only national experiment (now more than two decades old) is on a downhill slide.

Free radio and TV time for statewide and legislative candidates usually are associated with the advocacy of public financing of campaigns. Not bloody likely, in Texas or elsewhere, in today's political climate. First of all, that would have to be ordained under federal law, and that's almost surely dead meat in Washington. President Clinton's proposal to provide free airtime for campaigns in federal elections was killed outright by broadcast corporations. And a recent Center for Public Integrity study showed that, from 1996 to mid-year 2000, the 50 largest media companies and their related trade associations spent $111.3 million to lobby Congress and the federal executive branch — and the same groups, from 1993 to mid-year 2000, gave another $75 million to candidates for federal office and to the two major political parties. The largest single beneficiary? Sen. John McCain, R-Ariz., chairman of the Senate Commerce Committee, who collected more than $685,000 in media money — even while being a news media favorite, of sorts, for his advocacy of campaign-finance reform.

★   ★   ★

Finally, beware a cynicism that appears to be catching. Polls over the last few years show that half to two-thirds of Americans think their politicians are crooked in some way, or must be, and up to 9 out of 10 will say that something needs to be done to clean up the election process. But at the same time, with or without those same cynics voting, 80 to 95 percent of incumbents — including most of those "crooks," I suppose — get re-elected. On the other hand, it may be that the continuing electoral success of those crooks is the reason people aren't going to the polls like they used to. Besides, cynicism is something like a mushroom: It grows best in the dark and covered by fertilizer. If citizens feel like something is broke but ain't getting fixed or can't fix it themselves, they seethe in frustration at the politicians—and that feeds on itself. At the same time, despite 40 years of watching Texas politics up close, I remain an optimist: Given the public's disinterest in elections and its reluctance to demand change, I still think the people of Texas get better government than we truly deserve. It can be made better, clearly, and that's why I wrote this book.

★   ★   ★

If, after also reading the interviews in Chapter 7, you are still curious about the reform chorus and you want more information, here's what to do and how to get it:

• Get on the Internet (www.ethics.state.tx.us) and check out the Texas Ethics Commission's new computerized system for checking campaign contributions (and expenditures). It's not yet as user-friendly as many computerized systems of information, but it has the added blessing of being current. For another source, or comparison, go to the Federal Election Commission (www.fec.gov) for reports on U.S. senatorial and congressional races.

• If that isn't enough information, or you want to move more quickly, go on the Internet to the National Institute on Money in State Politics (www.followthe-money.org), the Center for Responsive Politics (www.opensecrets.org), the Center for Public Integrity (www.publicintegrity.org) or Texans for Public Justice (www.tpj.org).

• Call, write or e-mail your Texas legislators. The Texas House is at 512/463-1000, or PO Box 2910, Austin 78768. The Texas Senate is at 512/463-0001 or PO

Box 12068, Austin 78711. Tell them how you feel about this or other issues. If you don't know who your Texas legislators are, go to www.capitol.st.tx.us, and use the "finder" on the left-hand side of the page. If you are going to express an opinion on campaign-finance issues, write your legislators at the addresses above and send a copy of the letter to your local newspaper. If you're in a hurry, e-mail House members to firstname.lastname@house.state.tx.us or Senate members to firstname.lastname @senate.state.tx.us.

And, if all of this information inspires you to be a more active political citizen, get registered to vote and get involved. If you've never participated in a campaign, do so. Start with a race for the city council or school board (both of which are nonpartisan ballots in Texas), or even for the Legislature, by calling a candidate's office. If you strongly identify with a political party, look in the phone book and get a local phone number to tell you how to get involved in that party's affairs on a local level. Go to the polls when votes are held. If you vote in the spring party primary elections, don't forget to go to the precinct convention that starts when the voting ends at 7 p.m., usually in the same building or one near-by.

AFTERWORD

★ ★ ★

C ampaigns for People believes that fundamental campaign reform is needed to decrease special interest power in Texas and that, contrary to much conventional wisdom, there is a real opportunity for reform. The public clearly wants reform. A 1999 statewide poll showed that 80% of Texans believe that the state's campaign system is corrupt and support major reform. This perception has been re-enforced by major corruption scandals involving officials in large Texas cities in the last several years. Major Texas newspapers have begun to speak out strongly for campaign reform, which was not true several years ago. A shift is also evident from the Speaker of the House's repeated calls for campaign reform, further raising the issue's public profile. Last, our organization's efforts, in building the first broad coalition in Texas for campaign reform, have improved substantially the ability to mobilize public support. For the next year, we are going to be focusing on "Open Campaigns," the need in Texas for full and timely disclosure of contributions before you vote.

We hope the average citizen gets involved in fighting to improve their democracy in Texas. You can let your legislator know how you feel about money triumphing over the public interest — especially since they say no one cares. You can also join our group in our non-partisan fight for reforms. To learn more, please go to our web site, www.campaignsforpeople.org.

I want to thank Sam Kinch Jr. and Anne Marie Kilday for all their hard work and producing a wonderful book. I also want to thank the Deer Creek and Trull Foundations for their grants that have helped to underwrite the book And last, but not least, I want to thank the Texans who care enough about democracy in Texas to get out there and work for change. We can make a difference.

Fred Lewis
Campaigns for People
November 2000
Austin, Texas

Steve Dodds - Alan's friend

- axes rd.
right on riverside
→ 3rd light congress
left (2 lights)
2nd light → Monroe
(left)
1st stop sign (newming)
1½ blocks, on right
- large house (yellow)
~~45~~ 419 or 420

$ in sports + politics